Free in Christ

Free in Christ

The New Testament Understanding of Freedom

Warren McWilliams

BROADMAN PRESS
Nashville, Tennessee

© Copyright 1984 ● Broadman Press
All Rights Reserved.
4216-09

ISBN: 0-8054-1609-9
Dewey Decimal Classification: 248.4
Subject Headings: CHRISTIAN LIFE—FREEDOM
Library of Congress Catalog Number: 84-2812
Printed in the United States of America

Library of Congress Cataloging in Publication Data

McWilliams, Warren, 1946-
    Free in Christ.

    1. Freedom (Theology)—Biblical teaching.   2. Bible.
N.T.—Criticism, interpretation, etc.   I. Title.
BS2545.F7M39 1984   261.7   84-2812
ISBN 0-8054-1609-9

Dedicated to
Patty, Amy, and Karen

Contents

Contents

6. Live as Free People: Freedom in the General Letters

7. The Future of Freedom

Preface

Why did I write this book? Why should you read it? These are the two questions I think a preface should answer. I won't try to summarize the entire book here, but I want you, the reader, to know why I think this book was worth my time to write and your time to read.

Why did I write this book? Why would a white, adult male with a good job and a loving family be concerned about the themes of bondage and freedom? Certainly I have never been in jail or felt the oppression of racial or sexual discrimination. I can pretty well go anywhere or do anything I want—within some limits. Probably my main reasons for devoting several years of thought and energy to this subject—freedom in the New Testament—are two.

First, I have increasingly identified emotionally and psychologically with the oppressed minorities of our country, especially blacks, women, and native Americans. I grew up in the 1950s when these groups were (to my knowledge anyway) not very vocal about their bondage. In the 1960s and 1970s I saw a ground swell of concern for liberation. At first I was shocked by the arrogance of some of these liberation movements, but I gradually realized my own culture was racist and sexist.

Second, I became aware that the New Testament speaks very directly to the theme of liberation. In fact, the Bible as a whole often describes God as a liberator. God set the Hebrews free from their Egyptian bondage and in Christ he liberates us from our sins. After much study and reflection I became convinced that interest in the Bible and liberation are not merely compatible—they are intimately related. As a committed Christian I *had* to study the biblical teaching on freedom. But now I have begun to answer that second question as well.

Why should you read this book? Here again I have two reasons. First, I firmly believe that you as a Christian also have a duty to study the Bible to determine what it says about current issues. As Christians we believe the Bible is relevant to all of the concerns of life. I offer to you a topical study. I realize, however, that topical studies can be dangerous. A concordance approach to a subject might give you all of the passages that deal with topic *X* or subject *Y* or issue *Z*, but you could easily ignore the historical and cultural context of the passage. Although I have taken the topic of freedom, I have also chosen to study it by looking at each major block of New Testament material, analyzing that material in light of its historical background. At the end of our study we can more safely draw some conclusions about the New Testament view of freedom.

Second, I believe this book fills a gap in current discussions of the subject. In a day when thousands of books pour off the presses, little is being said about the biblical view of freedom. If you checked some bibliographies on freedom, you would find that there has been a flood of literature on freedom and even liberation theology in the last decade or so. There have been relatively few studies of the biblical witness, however, and these are usually written for the scholar or for a non-American audience.

In this work I have tried to state the New Testament understanding of freedom in clear, nontechnical language. I have not burdened my discussion with the usual scholarly jargon or documentation although I have tried to reflect the consensus of New Testament scholarship. I have learned much from other books which will be obvious to a scholar. My main goal, however, is to give the interested layperson an intelligible overview of the New Testament interpretation of freedom.

After an introductory chapter which reviews some of the current discussion of freedom and summarizes the rival view of freedom at the time of Jesus, each chapter treats a block of biblical material. The last chapter will especially try to draw some lessons for us from this study although the relevance of the New Testament teaching will be a concern throughout our study.

I know the reader of prefaces is often bored by a long list of acknowledgments, but I must express my gratitude to several people. My colleagues at Oklahoma Baptist University have been very encouraging to me. The members of University Baptist Church have often let me see how a local congregation struggles with the burden of freedom in the contemporary world.

My thanks go to Sherri Stoddard who gave up part of her summer to type this book. Three of my former teachers may see their influence on me in this work: James Timberlake of Oklahoma Baptist University who introduced me to New Testament Greek; David Mueller of The Southern Baptist Theological Seminary who introduced me to the study of theology; and Peter Hodgson of Vanderbilt University who impressed me with his study of the theology of freedom.

My wife, Patty, and my daughters, Amy and Karen, have contributed in so many ways to my personal freedom. Over and over again they have incarnated the liberating love of God for me. To these three women I dedicate this book.

Warren McWilliams
Oklahoma Baptist University
Shawnee, Oklahoma

1
The Struggle for Freedom

Try an experiment. Ask ten of your friends what they want most out of life. Their answers will probably include money, happiness, fame, and good health. If you then asked them why they wanted these things, their replies would quite likely include some expression of a desire for freedom. We often want money in order to be free from poverty and to be free to do whatever we want to do or go wherever we want to go. We might want happiness because it means freedom from worry, tension, anxiety, and depression. Fame could liberate us from feelings of insignificance and futility. To be in good health involves freedom from pain, disease, and ultimately the fear of death. Almost all of our deepest desires entail freedom. If freedom is not the most fundamental human yearning, it at least is a pervasive human concern.

This desire for freedom provides a bridge between the late twentieth century, our world, and the first century AD, the world of Jesus. In this chapter our concern is to sketch the struggle for freedom in these two time periods. Since freedom is a goal for most human beings, it will not be surprising that there are clear similarities between these two periods.

The Contemporary Debate

The twentieth century has seen an explosion of interest in freedom. Politicians guarantee that their programs of legislation will give us all the freedom we want. Psychologists such as B. F. Skinner tell us we need to go *Beyond Freedom and Dignity*. Psychiatrists want to liberate us from our anxieties and hang-ups. Self-help authors want to set us free from our economic worries. Creators of the wonders of technology offer liberation from the drudgery of routine tasks.

God or Freedom?

Where does the Christian faith fit into this ferment of discussion about freedom? Many seem to have adopted the attitude of some of the ancient Hebrews: "Why then do my people say, 'We are free, we will come no more to thee'?" (Jer. 2:31, RSV). When everyone wants to be free, the choice seems to be: God *or* freedom. As one theologian noted recently, one of the most common types of atheism in our time is the atheism of human freedom.

Why do some people see belief in God and the pursuit of freedom as incompatible? One of the basic reasons for this either-or thinking is the image of God as an omnipotent being who manipulates human destiny. God becomes a despot who controls us like robots. Some biblical passages taken out of context seem to support this view of God. For example, Jeremiah's story of his visit to the potter's house (Jer. 18) has often been interpreted in a deterministic way. We picture God molding some clay, and the clay is totally passive.

Actually the story reveals a God who is infinitely patient and willing to work with the Hebrew nation. The potter keeps on working with the Hebrews because they are free enough to rebel. Only when they become hard and refuse to listen to God are they condemned (Jer. 19). Even in the New Testament the images of God as a master and of human beings as slaves reinforces this view of God as the divine tyrant. Paul uses the master-slave metaphor for the divine-human relationship, noting that our choice is to be a slave of sin or a slave of God (Rom. 6:20-22).

We will explore Paul's view in more detail later, but we must recall that Paul was using a word picture that would communicate better to his age than ours. On other occasions he stresses the freedom motif. Even some of our songs reinforce the perception that to be free is incompatible with loyalty to God. "I Surrender All," for example, would sound totally oppressive to someone outside the Christian faith.

The church also has an oppressive image for many contemporary Americans. This attitude is classically stated in Dostoevski's "The Grand Inquisitor." In this chapter from *The Brothers Karamazov*, the grand inquisitor confronts Jesus in sixteenth century Seville, Spain. According to the inquisitor, Jesus was foolish to offer human beings freedom during his earthly ministry. People do not want to be free; they want to be controlled. The institutional church has recognized this fact, and it has used "miracle, mystery, and authority" to control Christians.

While it is true that the church has been oppressive and legalistic at times, the New Testament accents how welcome the oppressed of the first century felt in the church. Indeed, Paul could argue that in Christ racial, sexual, and economic distinctions do not count (Gal. 3:28).

Our contemporary culture places the priority on autonomy rather than authority. "Autonomy" comes from Greek words meaning self-governed (*autos,* self, and *nomos,* law). Our cultural national anthem has almost become "I Did It My Way." When one's total orientation is self-motivation, self-direction, or self-actualization, criticism of any authority comes easy. To the autonomous individual submission to an external control, or heteronomy (*heteros,* other, and *nomos,* law), is totally unacceptable. Too often Christianity has been perceived as totally authoritarian and oppressive. During the European Enlightenment, for example, to be a "free thinker" was normally to be a critic of the institutional church.

Perhaps one way out of this autonomy/authority dilemma is provided by Paul Tillich, who compared autonomy, heteronomy, and theonomy. Tillich suggested that theonomy (*theos,* God, and *nomos,* law) is the healthiest approach, with us oriented to God's law. This law is not oppressive because we are God's creatures. Authority becomes restrictive or enslaving only when it is arbitrary or capricious. God's law actually encourages self-actualization because God created us and wants what is best for us. God's law "fits" us just as Jesus' yoke is "easy" (Matt. 11:30).

What Kind of Freedom?

Almost everyone would agree that freedom is important. Indeed, our constitution suggests that as Americans we have a "right" to liberty along with life and the pursuit of happiness. Yet we don't always agree on what freedom is *or* how to achieve it. For the sake of brevity, we will focus on some of the most prominent freedom movements of our time rather than attempting a comprehensive catalog of definitions of freedom.

Many contemporary liberation movements are concerned primarily with *political-economic* freedom. This concern arises when some aspect of our public, social life is restricted by prejudice, limited resources, or legislation. The civil rights movement of the 1960s, for example, was a protest against racism. Blacks spoke out for legislation that would guarantee equal job opportunities, education, open housing, and other basic civil rights. Anyone who watched the evening news in those years remembers the chants of "Black is beautiful" and the sight of marchers singing "We Shall Overcome."

The women's movement is very similar to the black movement. Women identified sexism as a parallel form of prejudice that affected basic human rights. Again there were protest demonstrations and demands for legislative solutions to this type of bondage. One other liberation movement with parallel concerns includes senior citizens who protest ageism or prejudice against older people. Here again legislation and social reform are perceived as essential to freedom.

Although most protesters against racism, sexism, or ageism in this country are prepared to work with the legislative process, some extremists move toward more radical social reform. Some even propose violence and political revolution.

Although political-economic freedom is a basic concern of our time, some people are more interested in *emotional-psychological* freedom. These people feel more oppressed by psychological anxieties or disorders than external, social restrictions. Rather than seeking legislative solutions to their bondage they turn to therapy or drugs for release. They perceive freedom as being private and internal rather than public and institutional. Of course this concern for psychological liberation does not exclude political-economic liberation. Feminists, for example, often form "consciousness-raising" groups to give emotional support to women while also lobbying for political remedies.

Some people are so preoccupied with their individual concerns, however, that they privatize freedom and ignore the public world. Some young people, for example, turn to drugs, mysticism, or eastern religions in an attempt to be free from some slavery. In the 1960s and early 1970s the hippie counterculture developed partly because of this desire to drop out of an oppressive mainstream culture. Today middle-class business people often find it easier to find freedom in a bottle of whiskey than in trying to change the world.

One other prominent form of freedom deserves attention. *Rational-scientific* freedom involves the attempt to understand a complex world and control it through technology or education. Modern technology has liberated us from so many unpleasant aspects of life, yet we often take it for granted. Perhaps you can get a glimpse of the benefits of modern technology if you imagine what your daily life would have been like only 200 years ago. Indoor plumbing, bypass surgery, computers, television, hybrid grains, and so much more would disappear. The development of modern science with its dual concern to understand and to control the physical world has liberated us from much.

Gradually we are realizing, however, that technology has some liabilities. The same technology that liberates can also enslave. Television, for example, provides us with information and entertainment, but we have become passive spectators rather than active participants. We watch a concert instead of learning to play a musical instrument. In fact many people are as strongly addicted to television and video games as junkies are addicted to drugs. Still, modern technology liberates us from some of the physical stresses that enslaved earlier generations. In many ways we are freer from disease, hunger, and isolation than our grandparents, although we may be destroying our environment.

These three forms of freedom, and others, are prominent in our culture. In each case some type of oppression is identified as the basic form of human slavery. Freedom is defined as release from racism or sexism or ageism or anxiety or the struggle for survival. The method for gaining freedom varies: politics, social reform, drugs, therapy, or technology.

Although our discussion of these rival freedoms has been purposely sketchy, one further comment seems appropriate. As we will see in a later chapter, the New Testament does not negate any of these types of freedom as being intrinsically wrong. Christians can legitimately pursue political-economic freedom, emotional-psychological freedom, and rational-scientific freedom. Christians, however, know that these types of freedom do not exhaust the biblical perspective on freedom. The Bible points to a freedom that encompasses yet transcends these other dimensions.

The Bible and Freedom?

Several years ago a writer said he put a paper clip on every page in the New Testament that dealt with freedom. Almost every page had a paper clip! Although the primary Greek word for freedom may not be on every page, the concept is very common in the New Testament. Jesus was the liberating Lord, and early Christians were convinced that true freedom came through him.

Before turning to the first-century background for the New Testament view of freedom, perhaps a few comments on interpretation are appropriate. Our concern here is to remind ourselves of some important factors in proper interpretation. Proper interpretation involves understanding the historical context of of a passage—the literary form (poetry, parable, riddle, etc.), the meaning of key words ("grace," "freedom," "sin," etc.)—using the best translations, and following the guidance of the Holy Spirit.

In this study we will try to look at the New Testament teaching on freedom in its proper context. Here I take "context" to mean two things: First, it may refer to the historical-cultural setting of a passage of Scripture. Every time we approach a text we need to ask what it *meant* to the original audience and what it *means* to us today. Too often we are so eager to see how a passage applies to our lives today that we overlook the necessary historical study that will give us a better understanding of the text. We need to remind ourselves of Philip's question to the Ethiopian man: "Do you understand what you are reading?" (Acts 8:30, NIV). The meaning of some passages may be fairly obvious, but often we need someone, like Philip, to guide us (Acts 8:31). In our study of the New Testament view of freedom we will be concerned to see the texts in their historical-cultural context.

Second, "context" may refer to the position of a text within a larger argument by a biblical author. I learned once that a text without a context is a proof text. We are striving to do proper interpretation (*exegesis*), but sometimes we do improper interpretation (*eisegesis*). I do not believe you can prove just anything from Scripture, but taking a text out of context can make Scripture very misleading. We can take a saying of Abraham Lincoln: "You can fool all the people some of the time." By itself, this statement leaves the impression that Lincoln was very cynical about human nature. But when you look at this quotation in the context of Lincoln's larger thought, it means just the opposite. Lincoln actually said, "You can fool all the people some of the time, and some of the people all of the time, but you cannot fool all the people all of the time." Lincoln actually had a high regard for our ability to discern the true from the false.

When we interpret the freedom theme in the New Testament, we need to keep the larger context of the author's overall argument in mind. In so doing, we will be close to the old principle of letting the Bible interpret itself. Knowing the historical context is essential, but equally crucial is considering the biblical author's train of thought.

That many biblical scholars and theologians are stressing freedom now is a cause of concern to some Christians. These Christians fear that so-called liberation theology may simply be an attempt to jump on the bandwagon of a primarily secular liberation movement. If, for example, a feminist theologian begins to quote biblical texts that suggest woman is not inferior to man, the theologian is accused of proof texting or eisegesis. We are so used to a male-oriented, hierarchical view of the Bible that any suggestion of more freedom for women must be wrong! In light of this concern, I will try to develop the teaching on freedom in light of the total message of the New Testament. Of course I cannot summarize the entire New Testament, but I will try to place a biblical text dealing with freedom in the context of the larger argument of the book as well as its historical background.

In conclusion, we have seen that there is considerable debate in the twentieth century about freedom and how to achieve it. Is the Bible, especially the New Testament, relevant to these concerns? As a Christian, I firmly believe the New Testament speaks to every concern of life. In the next section of this chapter, we will look at the struggle for freedom in the time of Jesus. Not surprisingly, freedom was a major concern for Jews and Gentiles in the Roman empire of the first century AD. Indeed, the struggle for freedom provides a natural bridge between our era and theirs.

Freedom in the World of Jesus

Everyone in the first century wanted to be free from something. Our concern in this section is to review briefly the major understandings of freedom in the New Testament era. We cannot be exhaustive here, but such a study is essential if we are to understand properly the New Testament message about freedom in Christ.

Hellenistic Views of Freedom

Freedom was understood from a variety of perspectives in the Roman Empire. Part of this diversity of opinion was due to the intermingling of Greek and Roman religions and philosophies in the Roman world. Although the Romans basically adopted the Greek or Hellenistic mentality on many subjects, they often modified the Greek viewpoint. Instead of tracing the development of these Greco-Roman viewpoints, I will highlight the major rival views in the first century AD.

Political Freedom

Many Romans considered themselves free because they were citizens. Not everyone in the Roman Empire was free, only adult males. Women, children, many foreigners, and slaves did not have the rights of a citizen. To be a citizen was to be free from preoccupation with the necessities of physical life. Slaves took care of these necessities for most citizens. A citizen was also free to speak in public and to act in public. To the Greeks a citizen (*polites*) was a free member of a city-state (*polis*), such as Athens or Sparta. According to Aristotle, a city-state was the "community of the free." The Greek philosophers might debate what specific form of goverment was best, but they all basically took the relative freedom of the citizen for granted.

Some, like Plato, were worried that democracy opened the door for the rule of an ignorant mob. Plato's ideal state, mapped out in the *Republic,* is an aristocracy ruled by philosopher-kings. Many Greeks and Romans were apparently disturbed about the possibility of anarchy if individual freedom went to an extreme. Individual *hubris,* or pride, was the major vice in much of Greek literature. The myth of Prometheus epitomizes this danger. Prometheus stole fire from the gods and was punished forever for his arrogance. In the political arena, laws were imposed to protect the rights of the state over against the individual.

This vision of freedom as citizenship was basic to the Roman Empire. All people in the Empire could be classified as citizens or noncitizens. Paul the apostle was proud of the fact he was a citizen and used that fact to his advantage on occasion (Acts 16:37; 22:25-29; 25:10-11). Paul realized, however, that a Christian's ultimate citizenship was not Roman (Phil. 3:20). Freedom to participate in the government is important, but Christian freedom involves more than citizenship. When we turn to the New Testament we will need to clarify this point, for it has a tremendous bearing on contemporary issues. For example, to what extent should a Christian be concerned with human or civil rights? How far should a Christian participate in contemporary liberation movements?

Freedom Through Self-Control

Some Romans were not so concerned with the political or social expression of freedom. Whether or not you were a slave or free, rich or poor, you could attain an internal private freedom. Even if you could not control the external, public world of politics, you could control your personal attitude or emotions. Such an approach was very common in the time of Jesus and was popularized by the Stoics.

Stoicism was begun about 300 BC by Zeno in Athens. It became increasingly popular as people in the Greco-Roman world felt that many of the circumstances of their lives were beyond their control. As one scholar noted, the Roman Empire eventually experienced a "failure of nerve." Stoicism became popular as people increasingly stressed inner freedom.

The Stoics' emphasis on rational control of yourself was not totally new. Plato had pictured the human soul as a charioteer (reason) trying to control two horses pulling the chariot. The Greeks generally felt that reason was the highest aspect of human nature. Reason must control the emotions or passions.

For the Stoics the ideal of human existence was *apatheia* (emotionlessness). You should strive to control your emotions rationally. If something happened to you (for example, breaking a leg) the event itself was neutral. The event became good or bad only in your personal judgment. You could not change the fact that you broke your leg, but you could control your emotional response to the accident. Without this rational self-control, you would remain enslaved to an emotion or passion (*pathos*). If you can rationally overcome your emotions, you can achieve individual self-sufficiency (*autarkeia*). No matter what happened to you externally, you could remain internally independent.

Our popular stereotype of a stoic as someone who can grit his teeth and bear it is not too far off target. Stoicism was popular because it provided a new kind of freedom. Some might even see a point of contact between Stoicism and Paul's comment, "I have learned to be content whatever the circumstances. I know what it is to be in need, and I know what it is to have plenty. I have learned the secret of being content in any and every situation, whether well fed or hungry, whether living in plenty or in want" (Phil. 4:11-12, NIV). On the surface Paul was simply reaffirming the rational optimism of the Stoics.

The next verse reveals, however, that Paul's contentment (*autarkes,* self-sufficient) was not due to the victory of mind over circumstances: "I can do everything through him who gives me strength" (4:13, NIV). Paul had learned that true freedom comes not from self-sufficiency but from God-sufficiency. Paul was also aware that the real conflict is often not between our mind and the world but within ourselves. Controlling yourself is not so easy after all (Rom. 7:15-20).

If we examined the full teaching of the Bible, we would probably find that the proper attitude toward the circumstances of life is closer to Reinhold Niebuhr's famous "serenity prayer" than to Stoicism. "God grant me serenity to accept the things I cannot change, courage to change the things I can, and wisdom to know the difference." The Stoics looked for freedom only in serenity or "apathy," yet sometimes we can change our circumstances. Christians are free to live responsibly in their world. We are not commanded to accept the status quo. Adjustment or coping may be a modern psychological version of the Stoic attitude, but the Christian faith often encourages us to change the world rather than conform to it (Rom. 12:2).

Freedom from Anxiety

Another philosophy that experienced considerable success at the time of Jesus was Epicureanism. Begun about 300 BC by Epicurus, this philosophy was not as popular as Stoicism, but it too offered a different, welcome way to freedom. Epicureanism is often caricatured as an "eat, drink, and be merry" approach to life. Epicurus did say that the goal of life was the pursuit of pleasure and the avoidance of pain. Technically, Epicureanism was a philosophy of pleasure, or hedonism, somewhat like the beer commercial that urges us to live life with "gusto." Epicurus, however, encouraged prudence and enlightened self-interest instead of orgies and gluttony.

The real concern of Epicurus was not physical pleasure but psychological tranquility or peace of mind (*ataraxia*). You cannot be really happy if you are disturbed or upset. Much like the Stoics, Epicurus was looking for a way to cope with a world that was increasingly frustrating and overwhelming. If you could not be sure of much positive pleasure, you could at least avoid anxiety or worry.

Epicurus insisted that if one could overcome some basic fears or anxieties, contentment or tranquility would be possible. The two most common fears were: fear of the gods and fear of death. The Greeks and Romans frequently feared their gods because they were portrayed as immoral and capricious beings. Some of the Greek poets and philosophers had begun to criticize the traditional religion because of the immorality of the gods. Epicurus's solution was more far-reaching. We do not need to worry about the gods interfering in our lives because the gods are not at all interested in human affairs. You can live your life in the confidence that these gods will ignore you completely. Epicurus was not an atheist, but he believed the gods were totally detached from human history.

The fear of death is probably a universal human apprehension. Most people probably are anxious about death because of the fear of the unknown or the fear of possible suffering in the afterlife. Epicurus's response was that death is the end of human existence.

There is no afterlife; there is only nothingness. Both body and soul are composed of atoms and cease to exist at death. Because of this denial of afterlife, Epicurus could encourage his followers to focus their attention on living life to its fullest here and now.

The freedom from worry or anxiety offered by Epicurus was appealing to many in the Roman Empire. Indeed all of us would love to have a worry-free life. Rather than suggesting a total suppression of emotions, the Epicureans encouraged a prudent, enlightened pursuit of pleasure. Freedom from worry is approached differently in the New Testament. Jesus also tells us not to worry, but the motivation now is not resignation to a world beyond our control. For Jesus our peace of mind comes from the assurance that God is concerned about us, not that he is detached and unconcerned (Matt. 6:25-34). Death is not a source of anxiety to the Christian because of the assurance that the life after death is communion with God. In fact, Paul could even look forward to death (Phil. 1:21-24).

Freedom Through Release

Probably the most popular religious or philosophic movements in the Roman Empire in the first century were the mystery religions. By the time of Jesus the traditional religions of Greece and Rome were losing the devotion of the masses. The new worship of the emperor as divine was more of a superpatriotism than a bona fide religion. The mystery religions were extremely popular, however, and probably were the biggest rivals to Christianity.

The mystery religions had their origins in several countries. The Eleusinian cult appeared in Greece, Mithraism had its roots in Persia, the worship of Isis and Osiris flourished in Egypt, and the religion of Cybele originated in Asia Minor. Eventually, however, these new religions were available to almost everyone in the Roman world.

The mystery religions were popular for a variety of reasons. They appealed to the masses through their vivid retellings of myths, their elaborate initiation rituals, and their acceptance of all classes and genders of people. The primary attraction of the mystery religions, however, was the offer of personal immortality. Stoicism and Epicureanism liberated you from the world through reason or pleasure, but the mystery religions offered an ultimate or final release through immortality.

The mystery religions claimed the ability to give their adherents immortality because of their belief in a dying and rising god. Although the mystery religions differed in their details, each relied on the story of a god who died and miraculously came back to life. Because this god was victorious over death, his followers could participate in this victory over death. Although the ultimate release from the bondage of this life comes at death, participation in the rituals of a mystery religion gave a preliminary glimpse of this release. Through a brief ecstatic experience, something like a "high" on drugs, a devotee of a mystery religion could taste the freedom that would come to full expression at death.

Like Stoicism and Epicureanism, the mystery religions stressed a personal and private freedom. There was no impulse to change the world, only the yearning to flee from it. The mystery religions offered an ecstatic experience that allowed you to escape from the world, but you were not motivated to change the world. The Christian faith also points to some "mountaintop" or peak experiences, but these experiences should lead to an urge to change the world.

Perhaps a good example of this is the transfiguration of Jesus. After Jesus was transfigured on the mountain, Peter wanted to linger and savor this experience (Mark 9:5). Jesus led the disciples back down the mountain and began to heal the sick. The disciples who had not gone up the mountain were unable to heal the boy with an evil spirit. Perhaps they were impotent because they had not had the mountaintop experience.

The followers of the mystery religion wanted a steady diet of peak experiences without any involvement in the world. The disciples of Jesus learned that peak experiences are valuable, but there is more to Christian freedom than release from the world.

Jewish Views of Freedom

Although many claim that the concept of human freedom originated in Greece, the Jews had a long history of concern with the
reality of freedom. Our primary concern is with the rival views of
freedom in the Jewish world in the first century, but we must note
briefly the heritage of freedom in the Old Testament.

The Old Testament Legacy

Throughout their history the Hebrews had experienced God as
a liberator from bondage. The two greatest events in Hebrew history, the Exodus from Egyptian slavery and the liberation from the
Babylonian captivity or Exile, were freedom events. In both cases
God was the redeemer, the liberator. Whenever the Hebrews experienced oppression, they expected this liberator God to come to
their rescue. As they developed the concept of a messiah, they often
understood him to be a liberator who would set them free from the
political oppression of their day.

The Hebrews did not, however, always want to be free. For
example, as they left Egypt under the leadership of Moses, they
began to grumble about the lack of food and water. They were
learning that freedom is a burden and a responsibility. Several
years ago the psychologist Erich Fromm popularized the concept
of "escape from freedom." Fromm's concept seems to fit the Hebrew experience in the aftermath of the Exodus quite well. Initially,
they were glad to be free from Egyptian bondage, but now they
wanted to escape from their newfound freedom and return to
slavery. After all, there is a kind of security in slavery that sometimes seems more attractive than the insecurity or risk of freedom
(Ex. 16:2-3).

At times the Hebrews were politically free, but more often they
felt the enslavement of being an occupied land. On one occasion
the Hebrews felt political oppression so severely from fellow Hebrews that the nation split. In a reverse of later American history,
the north seceded from the south. About 922 BC Rehoboam suc-

ceeded his father Solomon as king. When he attempted to assert his authority over the northern tribes, they demanded liberty from Solomon's oppressive policies (for example, heavy taxes, slave labor). When Rehoboam refused to compromise, the northern tribes rebelled and formed the nation of Israel leaving the southern kingdom, Judah (1 Kings 12).

Later in their history the Jews sought religious and political freedom from the Seleucids. The Jewish revolutionaries were led by the Maccabees, and the story of their liberation movement is told in 1 and 2 Maccabees in the Apocrypha. First the Maccabees achieved religious freedom by capturing the Temple in Jerusalem, cleansing it of all signs of pagan worship, and rededicating it to the worship of God (about 168/167 BC). The annual celebration of this event is Hanukkah. Later the Maccabees were able to gain political freedom by defeating the Seleucid armies. For about eighty years (about 142-63 BC), the Jews were again politically free. In 63 BC they were defeated by the Romans, and the Jewish homeland was a politically occupied region throughout the New Testament period.

Here is one other comment about the Old Testament period. The prophets often spoke out in favor of freedom, focusing especially on economic and social oppression. The great eighth century prophets (especially Amos, Hosea, Isaiah, and Micah) criticized the rich and powerful for their manipulation and oppression of the poor (for example, Amos 2:6-7; 4:1-2; 8:4-6). Although the Hebrews often stressed freedom in terms of one's relation to God, as we will see later, they did not ignore the freedom that should characterize our relations with others.

As we turn to the Jewish world of the first century AD we need to remember that the Jews were not totally isolated from the rest of the Roman Empire. The ideas of the Stoics and others would have some impact on Jewish life. Our specific concern, nevertheless, is with the distinctive views of freedom in the Jewish world, the world where Jesus lived and taught.

Freedom Through the Law

The laws of God provided the basic orientation for Jewish life. Throughout their history the Jews saw freedom from the theocentric (God-centered) perspective. You were ultimately free because of your obedience to God's laws. The classic Jewish attitude toward the law and liberty is epitomized in Psalm 119:44-45 (RSV): "I will keep thy law continually, forever and ever; and I shall walk at liberty, for I have sought thy precepts." Such an attitude may seem contradictory or even absurd to many in the twentieth century, but it made perfect sense to a devout Jew. To the Jews their obedience of the law was based on gratitude, not a sense of legalism.

The law was given to the Hebrews at Mount Sinai *after* the Exodus. The Jews understood that the gift preceded the demand, the gospel came before the law. God set them free from bondage to the Egyptians. At Mount Sinai they willingly agreed to enter a covenant with God. These laws were not arbitrarily imposed on them. Rather they accepted them freely out of gratitude for what God had done for them.

I think this gift-demand pattern is implicit in the Ten Commandments. Before any commandment is listed God reminds them of what he has done for them: "I am the Lord your God, who brought you out of the land of Egypt, out of the house of bondage" (Ex. 20:2, RSV; compare 19:3-6). Because of their gratitude for God's deliverance they saw the law as a gift, not a restriction on their freedom, and they gladly accepted it. Indeed, all of Psalm 119 (quoted earlier), the longest psalm, is dedicated to this praise of the law.

Later in Jewish history, however, legalism began to develop. In the time of Jesus the Jewish group that best epitomizes this trend toward legalism was the *Pharisees.* We see the Pharisees in a very negative light because of Jesus' criticism of them for their legalism, hypocrisy, and arrogance (for example, Matt. 23).

The early Pharisees were motivated, apparently, by a desire to interpret the laws for each new generation. In this reinterpretation and application of the law, however, the laws became more complex and oppressive. The attempt to clarify and interpret led to a burdensome, oppressive legalism that enslaved the ordinary Jewish layperson.

For example, the Pharisees' interpretation of the commandment to remember the sabbath led to a list of thirty-nine kinds of work prohibited on the sabbath. This list included making a knot, untying a knot, writing two letters, lighting a fire, and sewing two stitches. Although the intent—clarification of the law—may be defensible, the result was the worst kind of legalism. By the time of Jesus, then, the law (plus interpretation) had become enslaving rather than liberating.

Later we will elaborate on how Jesus and Paul, in particular, evaluated the role of the law for the Christian. In brief, we can anticipate that they will criticize this later legalism while upholding the idea that gratitude for salvation should lead to a disciplined yet free life.

Christians today face the same dilemma as the Pharisees. We want to explain and apply biblical principles to our contemporary issues. On some issues the biblical witness may be fairly clear. On other issues, however, the biblical witness is not as clear as we would like it to be. The real danger is to turn our interpretations into legalistic rules binding on all Christians. Our concern for relevance can become a legalism just as oppressive as that of the Pharisees. Like the Pharisees, we may be guilty of neglecting "the weightier matters of the law, justice and mercy and faith" (Matt. 23:23, RSV). We may need Paul to remind us that the letter of the law kills but the Spirit gives life (2 Cor. 3:6).

Freedom Through Withdrawal

One Jewish group was so convinced of the wickedness of the world and the need for purity that they literally isolated themselves from the rest of the world. The Essenes are not mentioned by name in the New Testament, but we know of their existence from several sources. They are best known as the writers of the Dead Sea Scrolls discovered in caves on the edge of the Dead Sea in 1947. These scrolls were written within a century of the time of Jesus by Essenes living at Qumran. The first group was led to Qumran by a "teacher of righteousness" about 150 BC. The group wanted to escape the "wicked priest." They saw themselves as the true Israel, the faithful remnant of the Hebrews.

The theology of the Essenes was apparently very similar to that of the Pharisees, but they went to greater extremes than the Pharisees to be free from the contamination of Roman life. "Pharisee" probably means "separatist," but the Pharisees were willing to live in mainstream Jewish society and retain their identity by upholding the letter of the law. The Essenes actually isolated themselves geographically as well as emotionally from the corruptions of society. In many ways they tried to establish an ideal society, a utopia, where they would be free from the distractions of the world. They shared their resources, had common meals, conducted common worship, and were often celibate (single).

The attempt to be free by withdrawal was not new, even in Jewish life. Others, such as the Rechabites (Jer. 35) adopted a distinctive life-style and refused to participate in ordinary Jewish life. In our day many have tried to establish communes where they could be free from the distractions and restrictions of modern life. The countercultures of our day reflect this concern: the beatniks of the 1950s, the hippies of the 1960s, and the survivalists or doomsdayers of the 1970s and 80's who hoard food and weapons are good examples of freedom through withdrawal.

The concern to be free through isolation has some points of contact with the New Testament. For example, James tells us that pure religion involves keeping "oneself unstained from the world" (1:27, RSV). John tells Christians that they must flee the wicked "Babylon" before it is destroyed: "Come out of her, my people, lest you take part in her sins, lest you share in her plagues" (Rev. 18:4, RSV).

Overall, however, I believe the New Testament's major emphasis is that Christians are to be in the world but not of the world (John 17:15-16). Jesus talked of Christians being salt and light influencing the world, rather than fleeing the world to the security and freedom of some religious ghetto (Matt. 5:13-16).

Freedom Through Compromise

The *Sadducees* found yet another route to freedom, the way of compromise or expediency. They are unusual in that they were very conservative theologically yet very liberal politically and socially. It is in terms of their political attitudes that we see them finding freedom through compromise.

Theologically, the Sadducees were close to being the "fundamentalists" of their day. At least they liked to accuse the Pharisees of developing new, modernistic doctrines such as belief in resurrection of the dead. The Pharisees were willing to develop such beliefs even though there was minimal evidence in the Hebrew Bible (Old Testament). The Sadducees insisted on holding only those beliefs that were clearly expressed in Scripture, especially the law. They were also suspicious of the constant reinterpretation of the law done by the Pharisees because that oral tradition, or the tradition of the elders, threatened to rival the written Scripture for authority.

Despite this theological conservatism, the Sadducees were able to get along quite well with whomever was in political control of the Jewish nation. Most of the Sadducees came from the wealthy, priestly families that were used to being in power. If the Romans or some other group were in power, then the Sadducees could survive through whatever compromises were necessary. Throughout most of the first half of the first century AD most of the high priests were from the Sadducees. In order to survive, the Sadducees had to collaborate with the Roman procurators.

Although Jesus was apparently very critical of both the Pharisees and Sadducees during his ministry, the Sadducees seem to have been more opposed to the early Christian movement. When the Jerusalem church was persecuted by the Jewish religious leaders of all the religious groups the Sadducees were normally singled out for special reference (Acts 4:1-2; 5:17-18). They would have objected to the content of early Christian preaching because the claim of the resurrection would be absurd to them. Beyond that, the Sadducees would have objected to Christian preaching disturbing the peace. The large crowds that gathered in the Temple area would have been a threat to the public order.

The Sadducees, including the high priest, felt compelled to try to suppress this new movement before it attracted too much attention from the Roman officials. The Christians, like Christ, were likely to rock the boat. Jews such as the Sadducees who were simply trying to make the best of a bad situation, Roman occupation, could not tolerate such disturbances.

As an outside observer, it is easy to criticize this type of freedom. All of us say we would stick to our principles rather than compromising them. As a matter of fact, many of us daily make small adjustments in our moral principles in order to avoid unnecessary social embarassment. For example, none of us would in principle condone lying, yet we often tell small polite or benevolent lies. That is, we say we feel "fine" when we have a splitting headache, or we stretch the truth because the other person is not prepared for the unvarnished truth.

For most of us *compromise* has been a forbidden word. Christians do *not* compromise. To anticipate, Paul seemed to suggest that on some peripheral issues such as eating meat offered to idols, Christians should be willing to compromise! In an age when expediency is a way of life for many, any suggestion that compromise would ever be appropriate is dangerous. Certainly one can stay out of trouble in some situations because of compromise, but is this really freedom?

Freedom Through Revolution

The Jews that would have protested the loudest against the compromise of the Sadducees were the *Zealots*. The Zealots were the political revolutionaries of the first century. The earlier Maccabean revolt had begun as a spontaneous, grass-roots rebellion against the Seleucids. The Zealots appear to be a more solidified movement. They were Jewish superpatriots willing to use violent means to gain freedom from the Romans.

The first explicit references to the Zealots as a political movement are related to the revolt of 66 AD, but the Zealots were probably involved in a revolt in 6 AD led by Judas the Galilean (Acts 5:37). The revolt of 66 AD attracted the most attention from the Roman Empire. By 70 AD the Roman armies had almost defeated the rebels, but about 950 of the Zealots and their sympathizers fled to Masada, a fortress near the Dead Sea. The Roman army surrounded the fortress in 73 AD and captured it. Almost all the people were dead, apparently having agreed to kill each other rather than be captured by the Romans.

To paraphrase a twentieth century slogan, the Zealots thought they would be "better dead than Roman." The resistance of these patriots at Masada became legendary in Jewish history, and "Masada" has an emotional connotation to it much like the Alamo has for people in the southwestern part of the United States. Certainly the defenders of Masada approximate Patrick Henry's famous "Give me liberty or give me death."

Much has been written about the possibility of Jesus' contact with the Zealots. One of the twelve disciples was Simon the Zealot (Luke 6:15). Whether he was a Zealot in the sense of a political revolutionary or a zealot in the sense of an enthusiastic Jew is not clear. There is some speculation about the background of Judas Iscariot. Some scholars wonder if Iscariot might be derived from *sicarius* (dagger) rather than being the name of Judas' hometown (man of Kerioth).

Several recent fictional versions of the life of Jesus have hinted that Judas betrayed Jesus because of his frustration with Jesus' nonpolitical aspirations. Judas may have felt he could force Jesus into beginning a revolution by placing him in a confrontation with the Roman officials. According to this theory Judas was really trying to help Jesus, and Judas killed himself when he realized he had totally misjudged Jesus.

Another possible Zealot important in Jesus' life was Barabbas. Barabbas quite likely was not an ordinary robber but a political revolutionary (Mark 15:7). The choice between Jesus and Barabbas presented to the mob was really a choice between two approaches to freedom from the Romans: political revolution *or* nonviolent resistance. We will not try to infer too much from this meager evidence, but Jesus' attitude toward violence and political revolution will be important to our later discussion.

Equally well-meaning Christians have come to opposite conclusions about the appropriateness of violence. Some German Christians, for example, felt that the assassination of Hitler was permissible. Martin Luther King, Jr., however, based his nonviolent resistance of segregation laws on the teaching of Jesus.

Will the Real Freedom Please Stand Up?

As a child I liked to watch the television game show "To Tell the Truth." Three contestants would all claim to be John Doe. A panel of four celebrities would ask questions hoping to discover the real John Doe. At the end of the interrogation, the master of ceremonies would ask, "Will the real John Doe please stand up?" I remember the suspense as I waited for the real John Doe to be revealed.

By now you may be wondering which kind of freedom is the real or best freedom! In the first century and in the twentieth century people wanted and still want to be free. Many people are still waiting for the real freedom to stand up. Christians believe that true freedom is available only in Christ. To say that Christian freedom is true freedom is not to reject all of the perspectives we have reviewed in this chapter. In fact, Christian freedom has many facets and encompasses the best of the other views of freedom. A Christian is not limited to a narrow religious or spiritual conception of freedom. As we will see later in this book, Christian freedom is the richest, most profound kind of freedom. All other views of freedom are actually imperfect imitations or anticipations of Christian freedom.

In the next chapter we will begin to explore the New Testament understanding of freedom. Having seen the first century context, we can see how the freedom Jesus offers is more satisfactory than any freedom available then in the Roman Empire and anticipates the concerns of the twentieth century. In this first chapter we have seen that freedom is a major concern of human beings then and now. I am reminded of the title of Tom Skinner's book, *If Christ Is the Answer, What Are the Questions?* What is real freedom? How can I be truly free? Questions such as these are important to everyone. In the remainder of this work we will see how Jesus is the ultimate answer to these questions.

Study Questions

1. What kind of freedom or bondage is most vivid in your life?
2. Which kind of freedom is most sought by the people you know best?
3. Do people really want to be free *or* do they try to escape from freedom?
4. Would you agree with the grand inquisitor that the institutional Church has used "miracle, mystery, and authority" to suppress freedom?
5. If you were a Jew in the first century, which group would you join (Pharisees, Sadducees, Zealots, Essenes)?
6. Without looking ahead in this book, what made Jesus the totally free person?

Suggestions for Further Reading

Dostoevski, Fyodor. *The Brothers Karamazov.* New York: Random House, 1929.

Fromm, Erich. *Escape from Freedom.* New York: Farrar and Rinehart, 1941.

Josephus. *The Wars of the Jews.* In *Josephus: Complete Works.* Trans. by William Whiston. Grand Rapids, Mich.: Kregel, 1960. Book VIII, Chapters 8-9 discuss Masada.

Hodgson, Peter C. *New Birth of Freedom.* Philadelphia: Fortress Press, 1976. Chapters 1 and 2 especially.

Muller, Herbert J. *Freedom in the Ancient World.* New York: Harper, 1961.

2

To Set at Liberty:

Freedom in the
Synoptic Gospels

Son of God, Lord, Savior, Son of man, Messiah—these are some of the titles we normally use for Jesus. In the last few years several authors have suggested that another title should be revived: liberator. I say "revived" because there is abundant biblical evidence of Jesus as liberator. The liberation movements of this century have reminded us, however, that Jesus was indeed pro freedom and liberated people from several forms of oppression.

One reason we have neglected seeing Jesus as a liberator is that the language of freedom is not prominent in the Gospels. If you, for example, checked a concordance to the New Testament looking for "freedom" or "liberty," you would find almost no references in the Gospels. In John's Gospel Jesus promises to give his disciples the truth, and this "truth will make you free" (John 8:32, RSV).

The only explicit use of the main Greek word for freedom (*eleutheria*) in the other Gospels is in Matthew, where Jesus and his disciples are discussing the Temple tax. Jesus uses the Greek word for freedom here in the sense of exemption from responsibility to pay the tax (Matt. 17:26).

Although the Gospel writers do not use the term *freedom* very frequently, the reality of Jesus' liberating teaching and ministry is abundant. The title for this chapter comes from Luke's account of Jesus' inaugural sermon at Nazareth. Jesus chose a text from Isaiah 61:1-2 that includes an emphasis on his ministry of liberation:

The Spirit of the Lord is upon me, because he has chosen me to bring good news to the poor. He has sent me to proclaim liberty to the captives and recovery of sight to the blind, to set free the oppressed, and announce that the time has come when the Lord will save his people" (Luke 4:18-19, GNB).

Jesus' text indicates clearly that he came "to proclaim liberty" and "to set free the oppressed."

In this chapter we will, for the sake of clarity, divide our discussion into two sections, the first on the teaching of Jesus and the second on the ministry of Jesus. This division is artificial, but it is a traditional way of organizing treatments of Jesus.

Before we look at Jesus' teaching, we need to see why we are limiting our discussion to the Gospels of Matthew, Mark, and Luke. These three Gospels are frequently called the Synoptic Gospels. Synoptic refers to seeing ("optic") with a common viewpoint. The understandings of Jesus' life in the Synoptic Gospels are so similar that scholars generally treat them together.

The Gospel of John, probably written later, has a distinctive view of Jesus and will be discussed in the next chapter along with the other writings of John. Although the Synoptic Gospels are similar, they do have some distinctive emphases, including some differences in their views of liberation through Jesus' life.

In *Jesus Means Freedom,* Ernst Käsemann calls Mark's Gospel the "gospel of freedom," but each of the Gospels has its own emphasis on freedom. For example, Matthew accents Jesus' attitude toward the Jewish law. Jesus was, like Moses, a new lawgiver; yet his view of the law was not legalistic like that of the Pharisees. Mark emphasizes the action of Jesus rather than his teaching. He frequently stresses Jesus' personal freedom ("authority") and Jesus' ability to free people from demonic control (exorcisms). Luke's Gospel explores Jesus' openness to all kinds of people normally excluded from mainstream Jewish life (for example, women, sinners, lepers). In our discussion of the Synoptic Gospels we will generally not be concerned with these different angles of vision, but one could profitably study each Gospel separately, focusing on its distinctive portrait of Jesus as liberator.

To Proclaim Liberty: The Teaching of Jesus

Jesus rarely discussed freedom explicitly in his teaching, but his teaching introduces his disciples to a way of life that can be called liberating. In this section we will look at Jesus' teaching on freedom under two headings. First, we will focus on the major theme of Jesus' teaching, the kingdom of God. Second, we will look at the liberating message as presented through the parables.

The Kingdom of Freedom

The kingdom of God is the kingdom of freedom. Jesus never used the phrase "kingdom of freedom," but in the Synoptic Gospels he refers to the kingdom of God or kingdom of heaven over one hundred times. I believe the kingdom of God is Jesus' primary umbrella term for the new life one experiences as a Christian. To follow Jesus is to enter the kingdom of God. Since this new life is, as we shall see, a liberating experience, it may be fair to use kingdom of freedom as a synonym. If you follow Jesus, you are free.

What kind of freedom did Jesus offer through the Kingdom? The language of "kingdom" sounds odd to some people today because it suggests there is a king with servants. The main roots for the kingdom of God concept are in the Old Testament, where the Hebrews saw God as their king. If we have a king, how can we be free? Jesus uses the Kingdom language, but the king turns out to be a Father rather than a dictator. The Kingdom is a liberating experience rather than an enslaving one because the king is a loving Father rather than a malevolent despot!

We can better understand the Kingdom by answering two questions raised by people in Jesus' day. First, *when* does the Kingdom begin? The Jews wanted deliverance from the Roman oppression. They wanted freedom *now!* Sometimes Jesus spoke of the Kingdom being present (Matt. 12:28; Luke 17:21), but sometimes he spoke of it being still future (Matt. 6:10). His Jewish audience would have been perplexed. Jesus was suggesting that freedom was actual (present) and potential (future). How could that be?

Perhaps we can adapt an analogy from a contemporary scholar. Jesus' earthly ministry, death, and resurrection correspond to D-day in World War II, the real turning point of that war. Although there was more conflict, the definitive event had occurred. The return of Christ and the consummation of history corresponds to V-day in Europe. The German surrender and total realization of victory occurred after D-day. Between D-day and V-day many people experienced a tension between the "already" and the "not yet" of victory.

In a similar way, Jesus introduced true freedom through his earthly ministry, but the final realization of that freedom awaits the consummation of history.

Second, *how* is the Kingdom established? Ultimately, the kingdom of freedom is the kingdom of *God,* so we cannot establish it. As we saw in the first chapter, Jesus clearly opposed the violent revolution proposed by the Zealots as the way to freedom. Some of Jesus' actions could have been misunderstood as pro-Zealot actions, for example, the cleansing of the Temple and the triumphal entry into Jerusalem.

Some advocates of political and social revolution in our time have tried to argue that Jesus was a revolutionary of the Zealot persuasion. John notes for us that Jesus told Pilate that his kingdom was not of this world (John 18:36). Although Jesus was probably tried as a political criminal as well as a blasphemer, in fact he did not encourage political revolution as the way to establish his Kingdom.

Others have insisted that Jesus' kingdom was essentially an internal, private experience. Jesus did tell the Pharisees that "the Kingdom of God is within you" (Luke 17:21, GNB). This understanding of Jesus' kingdom is also misleading. The freedom Jesus offers is internal, but you are changed as a total being. Jesus did not encourage his disciples to escape from the world. He did not lead his followers to isolate themselves from the oppressive world in order to enjoy a purely private, mystical kind of freedom (Essenes).

Perhaps the best clue to Jesus' view of how freedom is established is his advice to be salt and light (Matt. 5:13-16). Because individuals have been liberated, they can have an influence on the world. We are salt and light, not dynamite. We can have a liberating influence on the world without withdrawing into our private freedom (Essenes) or by starting political revolutions (Zealots).

As we will see in our discussion of Peter and Paul, liberated Christians will need to be cautious in exercising their freedom if they are to have the best long-term impact on the pagan world. To use a crude example, Christians are to be thermostats rather than thermometers! Both devices measure the temperature in a room, but the thermometer leaves the temperature unchanged while the thermostat changes the situation.

The Parables of Freedom

Jesus' primary method of teaching was parables. Simply stated, parables are comparisons of the Kingdom with some ordinary aspect of life designed to provoke a decision about your entering the Kingdom. Clarence Jordan, author of the "Cotton Patch" translation of parts of the New Testament, once compared a parable to a literary Trojan horse. The audience thought they were going to hear a nice story about mustard seeds, a farmer sowing, or some other innocent subject, but by the end of the story they are being invited to make a life-changing decision!

The parables are invitations to exercise your freedom: Do you want to be in the Kingdom or not? Jesus does not coerce or manipulate you through parables, so hearing and responding to a parable can be a liberating event.

Parables, in other words, are open-ended. You can choose your own ending: liberty or continued bondage. In this way they remind me of a series of children's books my daughter, Amy, has read in which you choose your own adventure based on decisions you make as you read the plot. As you read or hear one of Jesus' parables, you have the opportunity to choose to be free or to continue to be enslaved.

In this section we will examine six themes in Jesus' parables that relate to the freedom offered by Jesus. First, some parables stress our experience of *freedom from guilt* when we enter the Kingdom. Although these parables are about a Kingdom, Jesus frequently stresses the fatherly love of God. Luke records a series of these parables that accent the willingness of God to accept the sinner and forgive sins. These parables deal with the lost sheep, the lost coin, and the lost (prodigal) son (Luke 15).

The last parable really focuses on the forgiving love of the father more than the repentance of the prodigal son. The son tries to be free by leaving home, but he seems to have a one-sided definition of freedom. Freedom for the prodigal son seems to be only freedom from: parents, home, and duty. The father illustrates the positive dimension of freedom, especially the freedom for acceptance and forgiveness. He welcomes his son home and has a party.

As we enter the Kingdom we, too, realize that the song "Just as I Am" is correct. God does accept us just as we are. We do not have to save ourselves and present ourselves to God. Rather, God accepts us, forgives us, and changes us. Later we will see how Paul incorporated this freedom from sin and guilt into his description of the Christian life.

Second, we experience *freedom from despair and presumption* about the apparent failure of God's activity in the world. Undoubtedly some of the Jewish views of freedom we examined in the first chapter represent a sense of despair about the future. They had been enslaved so long that they withdrew from the world (Essenes), compromised their principles in order to survive (Sadducees), held on to the law (Pharisees), or decided to take their destiny into their own hands (Zealots).

In several of his parables Jesus reminds his audience that appearances can be deceiving. For example, the parable of the sower (Mark 4:3-8) describes the unproductivity of some of the seeds. The main point of the parable is that *despite* the apparent setbacks the Kingdom is present already. Later Jesus gave the parable of seeds growing by themselves (Mark 4:26-29). The seeds are not ultimately dependent on the farmer. The Kingdom, in other words, is God's business, not ours. Again, in the parable of the mustard seed (Mark

4:30-32) Jesus noted that despite its small beginning the Kingdom is assured of growth.

These parables speak to many of us who have experienced disillusionment over the apparent failure of some cause we supported. It seems we fluctuate between presumption and despair. Presumption is epitomized in the attitude of Prometheus, who stole fire from the Greek gods. Despair is represented by Sisyphus, who rolled a boulder up a hill only to see it roll down again. On one hand, we assume nothing is going to change unless we do it (presumption). On the other hand, we give up hope and resign ourselves if we can't do it on our own (resignation).

Jesus' parables liberate us from both despair and presumption. God's kingdom is on its way. We can participate in its growth, but ultimately it is *God's* kingdom. We should not give up or try to take things into our own hands.

Third, we have *freedom of access* to God. Many people seem to fear God rather than love him. The Jews had the idea of God as father (for example, Hos. 11:1-4). In his parables Jesus tried to liberate us from this fear of God and to the freedom of approaching God as our father. After Jesus taught his disciples the Model Prayer ("Lord's Prayer"), he told the parable of the man who needed to borrow some bread from a friend late at night (Luke 11:5-8). Although the friend is already in bed for the night, the friend will get up and loan some food.

Jesus' point is that God will be infinitely more willing to respond to our requests. In his interpretation Jesus recommends: "Ask, and you will receive; seek, and you will find; knock, and the door will be opened to you" (Luke 11:9, GNB). Later Jesus told the parable of the widow who persisted in pleading her case before an arrogant and irreligious judge (Luke 18:1-8). Eventually the widow wears down the judge, and he responds favorably to her case.

Jesus uses here a kind of reverse psychology. Surely God, whose character is exactly the opposite of this callous judge, will be very receptive to our pleas. Jesus wants us to feel free to approach God. There is always the danger of our trying to be "chums" with God, but Jesus clearly teaches that God is our father, not our grandfather. He is loving and gracious to us, but he deserves our worship and respect.

Fourth, we experience the *freedom of personal fulfillment.* Today we hear a lot about self-actualization or self-development. Some of this discussion is valuable, because we do need to have a healthy self-esteem if we are to contribute to society. Some of this discussion, however, borders on the worst type of self-indulgence and self-centeredness. Jesus' parables treat this desire we have for self-fulfillment: for example, the two short parables about the treasure hidden in the field and the pearl of great price (Matt. 13:44-46).

All of us are personally on a quest for meaning or direction to life. Sometimes we accidentally find what we need; sometimes we look for a long time before we find what we want. Either way we are searching. Jesus' message is that only the kingdom of God will ultimately satisfy this search. "But seek first his kingdom and his righteousness, and all these things will be given to you as well" (Matt. 6:33, NIV).

Augustine, the early Christian theologian, began his *Confessions* by noting that we are restless until we find rest in God. Many people today, however, experiment with all kinds of actions and ideas in a futile attempt to find freedom or meaning apart from God. I recall an old song about a person who tries all that life offers, but the only refrain is the question, "Is that all there is?" Someone who enters the Kingdom experiences the joy and liberation of personal fulfillment.

Fifth, we are *free from misplaced priorities.* Before we enter the kingdom, our sense of values is out of line. Only in the Kingdom can we see what is really important. Alfred Nobel, the inventor of dynamite, realized his values were misplaced when he read his obituary. When one of Nobel's relatives died, the newspaper accidently printed Nobel's obituary. He realized how he would be remembered and changed his life, including establishing the Nobel prizes.

Several of Jesus' parables point to common misplaced priorities. The parable of the good Samaritan describes value systems of three men (Luke 10:30-37). The priest and the Levite both had something more important to do than to help the wounded traveler. The Samaritan knew that helping the man by the side of the road demanded his immediate attention.

The parable of Lazarus and the rich man (Luke 16:19-31) deals with a man whose riches seem to have blinded him to those around him. He never helps Lazarus in his misery, and he apparently is concerned about the final destiny of his five brothers only when it is too late. The parable of the rich fool (Luke 12:13-21) also deals with the seductiveness of wealth. The fool's only value is money, and his whole life is geared to the accummulation and enjoyment of wealth.

Jesus reveals several people with misplaced priorities in his parable of the great feast (Luke 14:15-24; compare Matt. 22:1-10). In Luke's account people refuse to come because they have to examine a field, try out new oxen, or to remain with their new bride. Although none of these activities are bad in themselves, they represent lower values when compared with the supreme value, entering the kingdom of God.

Sixth, we are *free from misleading preconceptions* about who can enter the Kingdom. As we saw earlier, God is loving and gracious, forgiving sins. Many people feel that there must be some other qualifications for the Kingdom. Jesus shocked many of the religious and social leaders of his day with his choice of companions. In some of his parables he forcefully stated that God is free to welcome anyone into the Kingdom. In fact, some suprising people may be there. Some people may not be in the Kingdom who thought they would be (Matt. 7:21-23).

Jesus told the parable of the Pharisee and the tax collector "to people who were sure of their own goodness and despised everybody else" (Luke 18:9, GNB). The Pharisee brags about his religion, but the tax collector is truly repentant and is the one accepted by God.

The parable of the workers in the vineyard (Matt. 20:1-16) again reinforces our awareness of the freedom of God from our preconceptions. When the owner of the vineyard pays his workers the same wage, even though some only worked part of the day, some workers complained. The vineyard owner asks, "Don't I have the right to do as I wish with my own money? Or are you jealous because I am generous?" (Matt. 20:15, GNB). Some people were astounded and offended that God could be so merciful!

Jesus' interpretation of the parable of the two sons (Matt. 21:28-32) is even more explicit and startling to the religious leaders: "The tax collectors and the prostitutes are going into the Kingdom of God ahead of you" (Matt. 21:31).

These are some of the dimensions of freedom people experienced as they responded to the parables of Jesus. Although Jesus did not explicitly use the vocabulary of freedom, his message was a liberating one for his audience. An early church theologian once noted that Jesus not only announced the Kingdom, he was the Kingdom. Your response to Jesus' message was your response to the Kingdom. In Jesus' day or ours, the way to true freedom is through the kingdom of God.

To Set Free the Oppressed: The Ministry of Jesus

Freedom is like the weather. Everybody talks about it, but no one ever does anything about it! Jesus talked about freedom, but he also did something about it. In the last section we looked at some aspects of Jesus' teaching on freedom. Now we turn to Jesus' personal freedom and his liberating ministry. Ideally, we could trace the entire life of Jesus, noting the dimensions of freedom. Instead we will focus on two broad areas of concern.

Jesus' Personal Freedom

Normally you have to be free to liberate someone else. At least I have a hard time finding an example of someone who is enslaved who can liberate others. Jesus' followers and others were quite impressed with his personal freedom. The Synoptic Gospels frequently note the reaction to the personal authority of Jesus (for example, Mark 1:27; 2:12). People who observed Jesus realized he was not bound to traditional authority. He was his own man. He was free!

One of the key examples of Jesus' personal freedom was his response to the Old Testament law. His attitude toward the law was twofold. On one hand, he rejected the ultimate authority of the law for himself and his disciples. He would go beyond the law and seem to break the letter of the law on occasions. On the other hand, he came to fulfill the law (Matt. 5:17-20).

In the Sermon on the Mount Jesus more concretely revealed his attitude toward the law through a series of six comparisons. In each case he said, "You have heard . . . But now I tell you:" (Matt. 5:21-48). He was not being egotistical, although that is what the religious leaders of his day thought. He was reinterpreting the law, focusing on the internal motivation in addition to the external act.

For example, he insisted it is just as wrong for a man to look lustfully at a woman as it is to commit adultery with her. Through this reinterpretation Jesus was taking the law very seriously, but he was personally liberated from a narrow legalism. In his personal actions he seemed to break the traditional laws, but in fact he was simply trying to put the law in its proper place.

Jesus' disciples picked some wheat on the sabbath. The Pharisees criticized them for breaking the Commandment about the sabbath. Jesus cited the precedent of David eating holy bread and then concluded, "The Sabbath was made for the good of man; man was not made for the Sabbath. So the Son of Man is Lord even of the Sabbath" (Mark 2:27-28, GNB). Later, the Pharisees criticized Jesus' disciples for not ritually washing their hands before eating. Jesus turned the tables on them by criticizing their neglect of the command to honor parents.

The Pharisees were technically dedicating their money to God (Corban) in order to avoid supporting their elderly parents (Mark 7:9-13). In these cases and others Jesus pinpointed the original meaning of the law and rejected a legalistic, hypocritical observance of it as inadequate. We still need to learn from Jesus on this point. Too often we are legalistic in our view of the Christian life.

We become so concerned about reaffirming the rules that we forget the reason for the rules.

Several actions by Jesus irritated or shocked the religious leaders of his day. To them he was free to the point of being sacrilegious. For example, Jesus forgave sins. To the devout Jews, only God himself could do that (Mark 2:1-12). He felt free to eat with socially unacceptable people (Mark 2:15-17). As we will see shortly, his miracles and exorcisms demonstrated an authority over nature that amazed his followers.

Jesus' three temptations also illustrate his personal freedom. An insecure person often tries to achieve his or her goals through shortcuts. All of these temptations seem to revolve around the question of the kind of Messiah he would be. He was tempted by Satan to take different shortcuts to attracting followers and establishing his Kingdom.

First, Jesus refused to be an economic messiah, winning followers by providing food. Second, he refused to use his spectacular powers to entice the crowds. Third, he refused to worship Satan in order to gain a ready-made Kingdom.

The Grand Inquisitor in *The Brothers Karamazov* argued that Jesus misjudged human nature. He believed people want to be controlled by "miracle, mystery, and authority." Jesus wanted free, responsible followers, not robots. He was free and wanted his disciples to follow him freely.

Jesus' Liberation of Others

Because Jesus was free, he could liberate others. We could look at almost every encounter Jesus had and see some element of liberation there, but we will focus on four categories of people who needed liberation.

The Poor and the Rich

Jesus identified with the poor and needy of his day, and he frequently criticized the dangers of wealth. Jesus' sermon on the plain, for example, includes the promise of blessing for the poor and disaster for the rich (Luke 6:20-24). We have already seen Jesus' criticism of the rich for their misplaced priorities in the parables of the rich fool and the rich man who neglected Lazarus.

Many of the Jews in Jesus' day would have been shocked by his identification with the poor. The Jews traditionally believed that the righteous prospered and the wicked were poor (for example, Deut. 28:1-14). Of course, the experience of Job was an exception to this pattern, but normally one could argue that God rewarded the industrious, pious person. Several of the Proverbs, for example, suggest that prosperity and poverty are clues to the level of piety (Prov. 6:6-11).

Throughout the Old Testament there had been another stream of thought, however, which Jesus emphasized more: that God was concerned for the poor who were poor because of economic injustice. Several of the prophets criticized the economic manipulation of the poor by the rich (Amos 2:6-7; 4:1-2; Hos. 12:7-8).

Jesus recognized the enslaving, consuming power of the love for money. In his ministry he gave the rich the opportunity to be free from their greed. Some were liberated; others refused to be set free. The rich young ruler, for example, chose to remain enslaved to his money (Mark 10:17-31). This young man was a "good" man in the sense that he had observed the commandments in the Law. Jesus knew that the man's real bondage was to his wealth. When Jesus told him to sell everything he had and give it to the poor, he was not requiring that of all Christians. Jesus was encouraging this rich man to acknowledge his bondage as the first step in being freed from it. He chose to remain in bondage.

Zacchaeus illustrates liberation from greed (Luke 19:1-10). As a tax collector Zacchaeus had been able to accumulate great wealth, probably through overtaxing the people in Jericho. Luke does not tell us if Jesus required Zacchaeus to return his tax money, but Zacchaeus announced that he would return the money if he had cheated people (v. 8).

The proper attitude toward money and those with or without it is still a significant question for Christians. Many of us know of the enslaving power of money or the desire for it. The legend about King Midas illustrates the human predicament concerning money. Midas was so obsessed with his desire for gold that he wished everything he touched would turn into gold. Tragically he realized the terrible price of this wish's being fulfilled. How to be good stewards of our possessions is still a major concern for Christians. We can be *slaves* to our desires for money or we can be *stewards*.

Women and Men

Jesus' attitude and actions toward women must have been one of the most startling aspects of his earthly ministry. Jewish society had a long tradition of male domination. Although there had been many famous women in Old Testament history (for example, Sarah, Rachel, Ruth, Esther), women had a relatively low status in Jewish society. Most of the debate about the New Testament view of women has focused on Paul's writings, but the attitude of Jesus toward male-female relations is absolutely fundamental.

Jesus has been described as "woman's best friend." Many contemporary Christian feminists claim Jesus had a much more open view toward women than did Christians in later centuries. Our concern here is not to explore all aspects of the contemporary debate over women, but to simply catching a glimpse of Jesus' position on the male-female relationship.

In order to focus our discussion more sharply, we will primarily examine passages in Luke's Gospel about women. Luke highlights Jesus' openness to several minority groups, and his Gospel has been called the "woman's gospel" because of its emphasis on Jesus' interaction with women.

Luke's Gospel notes the significant role women played in the birth and early life of Jesus. He recorded the visits of Gabriel to Elizabeth and Mary, Anna's adoration of the baby Jesus in the Temple, and Mary's involvement in the trip to Jerusalem when Jesus was twelve years old.

Luke also mentions that Jesus performed miracles involving women. For example, he raised the widow of Nain's son from the dead (Luke 7:11-17). He raised Jairus's daughter from the dead and healed the woman who touched the hem of his garment (Luke 8:40-56). The miracle that perhaps epitomizes what Jesus did for women in his day was the healing of the crippled woman. She "was bent over and could not straighten up at all" (Luke 13:11, GNB). When Jesus healed her, she could straighten up. Women of any generation who are oppressed are "bent over," but Jesus liberates them to standing straight.

Jesus was not afraid to be seen in the company of women. Normally in Jewish society a woman could not carry on a conversation in public with any man except a relative. When a sinful woman anointed Jesus' feet during a dinner at the home of Simon the Pharisee, Jesus did not rebuke her. Instead he told a parable about forgiveness and complimented the woman (Luke 7:36-50).

Here Jesus allowed a woman to be near him, acknowledging that she was a sinner, and then he had the audacity to forgive her sins! This openness toward women was so radical that some women occasionally traveled with Jesus and supported Jesus financially (Luke 8:1-3).

Perhaps one of the strongest stories in support of Jesus' liberation of women is his visit with Mary and Martha in Bethany (Luke 10:38-42). Martha was disturbed that Mary was not helping in the kitchen. Mary was listening to Jesus' teaching instead of fulfilling the more traditional domestic duties of women. Jesus did not reject this traditional role but insisted that Mary's choice of activities was the "right thing" for her (Luke 10:42, GNB). Since Jewish women could not normally study the law with a rabbi, Jesus was suggesting a radical departure in allowing Mary to study with him.

Although we have already discussed Jesus' teaching, we need to notice that Jesus presented a favorable picture of women in his teaching. For example, he included the parable of the woman looking for the lost coin in his discussion of God's love. God is like the shepherd looking for the lost sheep, the woman looking for the lost coin, and the father waiting patiently for his lost son (Luke 15).

We often fail to realize that Jesus was comparing God's nature to a woman. Jesus even used a feminine image to describe his love for Jerusalem. "How many times I wanted to put my arms around all your people, just as a hen gathers her chicks under her wings, but you would not let me!" (Luke 13:34, GNB).

Just as women were very involved in the birth and early years of Jesus' life, so women were prominent in his last days on earth. The Gospel writers recorded their presence at the crucifixion, their plan to finish preparing Jesus on resurrection Sunday morning, and their recognition of his resurrection. Indeed, John's Gospel reveals that the first appearance of the risen Jesus was to a woman, Mary Magdalene (20:11-16).

We have seen that throughout his ministry Jesus broke down the barriers of gender that relegated women to a lower position in society. Many have been perplexed that writers such as Paul and Peter do not seem as positive in their view of women. In our discussions of Peter and Paul we will see some of the factors involved in their writings. It is obvious from the Gospels, however, that Jesus wanted, to use contemporary jargon, to free us from sexism or discrimination based on gender.

As one person noted, Jesus would have been an equal opportunity employer. Jesus' main concern was not to initiate a social revolution, but his teachings about and actions toward women certainly lay the foundation for a healthier attitude toward women in the home, church, and society. It would be unfortunate, indeed, if the church of today failed to recognize and implement this important contribution of Jesus' ministry.

Sinners and Outcasts

Jesus associated with all kinds of people. His behavior was seen as scandalous by the social and religious leaders of Judaism. Jesus was not bound to social convention, however, and he ministered directly to the most needy of his day. In a sense Jesus focused his liberating ministry on first century minority groups. We have already seen his liberating attitude toward women and the poor; here we will focus on his attitude toward lepers, sinners, tax collectors, and other nationalities.

The context for Jesus' ministry to these groups was his desire to liberate all of us from snobbishness or elitism. In the Sermon on the Mount he emphasized this nonjudgmental attitude by warning us not to neglect the beam in our eye while pointing out the speck in our brother's eye (Matt. 7:1-6). Although our minority groups might be different today, we too need liberation from this judgmental attitude.

Jesus often associated with and healed lepers who were the social outcasts of their day. Leprosy made one unclean, and you were literally ostracized from society. Normally one did not even want to come close to a leper, much less have any dealings with him.

One of Jesus' early miracles involved healing a leper (Luke 5:12-14). Later Jesus healed ten lepers as he traveled to Jerusalem. One of them returned to thank Jesus. Interestingly, he was also a Samaritan (Luke 17:11-19).

One of Jesus' most liberating acts was to eat meals with sinners. You can tell a lot about someone's character by their mealtime companions. Normally, a devout Jew would not share a meal with a known sinner lest he seemed to be condoning their behavior. Jesus scandalized many people by associating with these sinners and often sharing a meal.

As one scholar noted, to some these meals were a *disgrace;* but to Jesus they were an act of *grace.* Jesus called Levi (Matthew), the tax collector, to be a disciple and promptly joined Levi and other tax collectors and outcasts at a meal (Luke 5:27-32). Jesus encouraged his disciples to put the poor, sick, and blind on their invitation lists for dinners (Luke 14:12-14). Earlier we saw that Jesus visited Zacchaeus's house for a meal (Luke 19:1-10).

Jesus also tried to liberate people from racism or nationalism. His message was for all people, not just Jews. Jesus had no animosity toward Samaritans although they had long been alienated from the Jews. John records a lengthy conversation with a Samaritan woman (John 4), but the Synoptic Gospels also note Jesus' openness to Samaritans. Luke, for example, notes that Jesus made a Samaritan the hero of one parable (Luke 10:30-37). We can begin to realize the shock the parable of the good Samaritan must have had on Jesus' Jewish audience by imagining what would have happened not so long ago if a white Southern pastor made a black the hero of a sermon illustration!

Discrimination against minority groups is hard to overcome. In the past quarter of a century much progress has been made in our country to alleviate discrimination against blacks, native Americans, Chicanos, and others, but much remains to be done. Jesus still wants to liberate us from our prejudice against "them," whoever they may be.

Diseased and Possessed

Some of the most vivid illustrations of Jesus' liberating power are the miracles he performed. By these miracles he liberated people from disease, demons, and death.

The healing miracles liberated people from physical illness. If you have been physically, especially chronically ill, you realize how enslaving illness can be. Jesus liberated some people from their physical disease just as he liberated others from prejudice, greed, or poverty.

Jesus' exorcisms of demons demonstrated his power over the evil spirits. Most of us do not encounter demon possession in our everyday life, but we recognize that people suffer addictions that are enslaving in a similar way. One of the most famous exorcisms, the story of the demoniac of Gadara, illustrates another issue: the fragmentation of life. Jesus asked the spirit for its name, and the demon replied, "My name is 'Mob' " (Luke 8:30, GNB). Many people today have such divided, fragmented lives that they also need Jesus to liberate them by giving them a single purpose or direction for life.

Jesus also revived people from the dead. These revivifications demonstrate in a preliminary way Jesus' power over death. Jesus' own resurrection from the dead is often cited in the New Testament as the basis for our liberation from the fear of death and death itself (for example, Heb. 2:14-15). In the ancient world many groups offered liberation from death, but Jesus' own death and resurrection provides the only valid liberation.

Freely You Have Received, Freely Give

When Jesus was instructing the twelve disciples for one of their missions, he said, "Freely you have received, freely give" (Matt. 10:8, NIV). Perhaps this chapter has helped you to see a glimpse of Jesus as liberator. Much more could be said, of course, but the emphasis of the Synoptic Gospels is clear. For many of us the idea of Jesus as liberator is still somewhat foreign.

The rest of our study will be an effort to understand how other New Testament writers saw this liberating Jesus. As we look at Jesus the liberator, we need to recall that Jesus called us to do more than understand him. He also calls us to action. If you are free in Christ, what are you doing about it in your daily life? Freely you have received, freely give!

Study Questions

1. What is your favorite parable? Does it have any emphasis on liberation from bondage?
2. If you had lived in the first century, what kind of freedom would you have wanted or most needed to receive from Jesus?
3. If you were freed from prejudice toward minority groups, how would that affect your daily behavior (for example, eating meals)?
4. What is your favorite story of a conversation Jesus had? Is this person being liberated by his or her encounter with Jesus?
5. "Freely you have received, freely give." What does this principle mean for you? How could it be applied to your life?

Suggestions for Further Reading

Jones, Peter Rhea. *The Teaching of the Parables.* Nashville: Broadman Press, 1982.

Jordan, Clarence and Bill Lane Doulos. *Cotton Patch Parables of Liberation.* Scottsdale: Herald Press, 1976.

Stagg, Evelyn and Frank. *Woman in the World of Jesus.* Philadelphia: Westminster Press, 1978.

Sider, Ronald J. *Rich Christians in an Age of Hunger: A Biblical Study.* Downers Grove: Inter-Varsity Press, 1977.

Stephens, Shirley. *A New Testament View of Women.* Nashville Broadman Press, 1980.

3

The Truth Will
Make You Free:
Freedom in the Writings of John

As a teacher I visit many schools and colleges. Frequently I see the title of this chapter taken from John 8:32 (RSV) as a motto or slogan for these institutions. Unfortunately these schools often seem to suggest that any kind of truth is liberating in the same way that Jesus' truth liberates.

Education in general has as one of its goals the liberation of our minds from ignorance, but the context of this verse clearly points to Jesus as the ultimate liberator. "If you obey my teaching, you are really my disciples; you will know the truth, and the truth will set you free" (John 8:31-32, GNB). Jesus was not discussing the value of education in general but the liberating effect of his truth for his disciples.

In this chapter we will focus on the five New Testament books traditionally attributed to John, the son of Zebedee, brother of James, and one of the twelve apostles. Scholars are not agreed that this John wrote all or any of these books, but for our study we will not need to review all of this debate. Whether or not this John wrote them, at least they provide a distinctive and welcome description of Jesus as liberator and freedom in the Christian life.

For the sake of organization we will look at the Gospel of John and the three Letters of John together and focus on Revelation in a separate section. The Gospel and the letters seem to have a fairly unified view of freedom. Revelation approaches the issue differently and responds to a different historical situation. As in the Synoptic Gospels, the term *freedom* is infrequent, but the reality of freedom is basic to all of John's writings.

The Good News and the Gnostics

The Gospel and the Letters of John all seem to discuss the liberating ministry of Jesus in the context of a first century movement known as Gnosticism. Before looking directly at freedom in these writings of John, we should see what views he is implicitly rejecting. As we will see, some of these views are still with us.

Freedom Through "Knowledge"

Gnosticism was a movement that claimed to have a special, even supernatural knowledge of God. The term Gnosticism comes from the Greek word *gnosis* (knowledge). The Gnostics were more "knowledgeable" or "in the know" than other people. Later Gnostic writings from the second and third century (for example, *The Gospel of Thomas)* claimed to consist of secret sayings of Jesus not included in the four New Testament Gospels. For the Gnostics this special knowledge was essential to true liberation. In some ways this emphasis on a secret, liberating knowledge made Gnosticism similar to a mystery religion.

John's Gospel emphasizes that Jesus was not trying to hide his message from the public. Rather, John often noted that Jesus spoke openly about himself (John 18:20-21; 7:25-26). John is much closer to the Hebrew view of knowledge than the Greek or Gnostic view.

To the Hebrews knowledge, especially of God, was an orientation of the total person to God on a very personal and intimate level. Hosea, for example, insisted that the Hebrews were condemned because they did not know God (Hos. 4:6; 6:6). Presumably, most Hebrews would have affirmed intellectual belief in a supreme being, but they did not know God in an experiential, personal way. The Greeks, and apparently the Gnostics, saw knowledge as more intellectual and less personal.

John stands in the Hebrew tradition. If you know Jesus, you are transformed not just informed. A few years ago someone said the two biggest problems today are ignorance and apathy ("I don't know and I don't care"). Whereas the Greeks and Gnostics might focus on ignorance as the main problem, John realized that Jesus addressed both. Jesus liberates us from our ignorance and indifference.

Freedom from the "World"

One of the distinctive beliefs of the Gnostics was dualism, the belief that reality consists of two ultimate components. Generally the Gnostics emphasized the distinction between the spiritual and the physical. In terms of human nature this dualism meant that soul and body were two radically different types of stuff.

The Gnostics went further to say that the spiritual reality was inherently good, and the material reality was inherently evil. This moral dualism led them to assert that the ultimate goal of life was to liberate the soul from the body and the physical world. The secret knowledge they offered allowed some liberation in this life, but their ultimate liberation came with release from the world.

In the first century and later the Christian faith rejected this Gnostic dualism by affirming three basic doctrines: the goodness of creation, the resurrection of the body, and the incarnation of Jesus. John's writings focus on the incarnation. The context for John's emphasis on the incarnation is his twofold use of the term *world.*

On one hand, John records a neutral meaning of *world.* The world is simply the sum total of reality. It is not inherently good or bad. On the other hand, John refers to "world" in a negative way. When he does this, however, he never adopts Gnostic dualism. Certain very distinct features of the world are mentioned, for example, in 1 John 2:16 (NIV): "the cravings of sinful man, the lust of his eyes and the boasting of what he has and does."

John affirms that Jesus was really human. In the introductory verses of the Gospel and the first letter he emphasizes the physical reality of Jesus: "The Word became flesh and lived for a while among us" (John 1:14, NIV; see 1 John 1:1-2). This belief in the incarnation was totally opposed to the Gnostic dualism. Because the physical world was seen as evil, they could not acknowledge the incarnation. The divine could not be contaminated with the physical! Their view is called Docetism by scholars. Docetism comes from a Greek word that means "to seem or appear."

Jesus only seemed to be human according to the Gnostics. He was God masquerading in a human costume. John later makes belief in the incarnation one of the tests of being a Christian. "This is how you will be able to know whether it is God's spirit: anyone who acknowledges that Jesus Christ came as a human being has the Spirit who comes from God. But anyone who denies this about Jesus does not have the Spirit from God" (1 John 4:2-3, GNB; see 2 John 7).

The incarnation is ultimately a mystery for all of us, but it is a key doctrine of our faith. John's concern to affirm the humanity of Jesus should be ours. I recall reading a few years ago the question, "Did the baby Jesus have diaper rash?" The point was that we often forget Jesus was human as well as divine. We as Christians often come close to Gnostic dualism, either in our neglect of Jesus' humanity or an apparent disdain for the physical world. Because of doctrines such as the incarnation, creation, and resurrection we should have a deep concern for the well-being of the physical world. The condition of the natural environment, for example, should be a concern for Christians.

Christians do not want to be "worldly" in the bad sense of adopting materialistic values such as greed. William Temple was probably correct, however, when he noted that Christianity is the most materialistic of the world's religions in the sense of affirming the value of the physical world. Gnosticism promoted liberation through escape from the world. Jesus did not pray that God take the disciples out of the world but that they not adopt a "worldly" attitude (John 17:14-16).

The Liberated Life: The Gospel and the Letters

Often we present the Christian faith exclusively in terms of self-denial and taking up your cross. Although these are good biblical images, we need to remember that Jesus offers us life to its fullest or abundant life (John 10:10). As the old song says, we need to "accentuate the positive" sometimes. In the Gospel and letters, John frequently uses the term *eternal life* for the Christian's existence. The title of this section, "the liberated life," is an attempt to put the meaning of eternal life in a nutshell. Although the language of "liberated life" is not John's, perhaps a further examination of it will reveal its appropriateness.

John said that the purpose of his Gospel was to produce belief in Jesus, that "through your faith in him you may have life" (John 20:31, GNB), and that the purpose of his letter was "that you may know that you have eternal life" (1 John 5:13). For Jesus, to have eternal life was to be his follower. To have eternal life means to be in the kingdom of God in the Synoptic Gospels. To have eternal life is to have changed the direction of your life.

Although John mentioned eternal life or the liberated life throughout his writings, we shall focus on two key episodes in the Gospel to further introduce the concept. John 6 gives the most detailed account in the New Testament of the feeding of the 5,000. All four Gospels record this event, and it is the only miracle in Jesus' ministry recorded in all four. Apparently John saw this event clearly illuminating Jesus' mission. After the people were fed and satisfied, Jesus recognized that they wanted to force him to be their king (John 6:15).

Many of these people had the typical political, nationalistic view of the Messiah as one who would establish an economic paradise and meet all of their physical needs. Although Jesus wanted to alleviate human suffering, he knew that the deepest human needs are more than physical. He did not reject their physical needs; that would be the dualist approach. In his teaching after the miraculous distribution of food, he stressed that he was offering a food that never spoils. " 'I am the bread of life," Jesus told them. "He who comes to me will never be hungry' " (John 6:35, GNB).

Jesus offered both physical and spiritual nourishment. He never split the two into neat compartments (such as sacred and secular) even though he saw a clear priority. The liberated life is a life that recognizes the value of the physical and the spiritual. The Gnostics, like some Christians, neglected the physical needs of people.

Jesus' raising of Lazarus from the dead introduced another important aspect of eternal life. Jesus was close friends with Mary, Martha, and Lazarus of Bethany. By the time he arrived at Bethany, Lazarus was already dead. Jesus told Martha that Lazarus would come back to life. Martha assumed Jesus meant the future resurrection of the dead. Jesus responded, "I am the resurrection and the life" (John 11:25, GNB).

When Jesus spoke of eternal life, some people believed he referred only or primarily to the afterlife. Jesus did indeed include a future dimension to his teaching (John 6:40; 11:25). Equally important is his emphasis on eternal life as a present quality of life as well as a future quantity of life. To offer a person with a miserable existence *more* of the same thing would not be liberating. In fact, some people commit suicide to avoid more of business (or life) as usual.

To offer only life after death would come close to the Gnostic or mystery religion promise of liberation through immortality. Jesus' gift of eternal life was liberating because it included a truly meaningful, "abundant" life here and now and a continuation of this new kind of life after physical death. Jesus accented that eternal life was a new kind of life by using *zoë*, a much richer word than mere physical existence (*bios*, from which we get "biology").

Freedom from Sin

John, like Paul, saw several dimensions or aspects of freedom in the Christian life. Indeed these two writers are the real theologians of freedom in the New Testament, working out the significance of Jesus' liberating ministry for Christians. The liberated life is so rich in John's writings that we will need to focus on only a few of its features.

Jesus pictured sin as a type of slavery from which only he can liberate. He said that "everyone who sins is a slave of sin. . . . If the Son sets you free, then you will be really free" (John

8:34-36, GNB). The context for this statement was the Jews' resistance to Jesus' teaching concerning the woman caught in adultery. The religious leaders had challenged him to confirm the need to stone her to death. Jesus invited the ones without sin to throw the first stone at her. Everyone left, and Jesus told the woman he would not condemn her.

Although this story in John 7:53 to 8:11 is not in the best manuscripts, many scholars agree it reflects the teaching of Jesus on sin. His main concern was to forgive sinners and thereby liberate them from their sins. Some of the Jews, however, apparently thought they did not need forgiveness since they were descendants of Abraham (John 8:33). At this point Jesus told them they were indeed slaves to sin and in need of liberation.

John actually begins his Gospel by noting the removal of sins as a major concern of Jesus' ministry. John the Baptist described Jesus as the "Lamb of God, who takes away the sin of the world!" (John 1:29, GNB). If one is free from sins, then one is also free from judgment. Jesus told Nicodemus that whoever "believes in the Son is not judged" (John 3:18). Jesus confronted some Jewish leaders after healing the lame man and told them that whoever has eternal life is not judged (John 5:24). Jesus' main purpose is to save people rather than judge them, but those who refuse to acknowledge him are enslaved to their sins and judgment (John 12:47-48).

John's first letter deals at some length with liberation from sin. The Christian is liberated from the slavery of sin in the sense of sin's total control of his or her life. Jesus has cleansed us from our sins (1 John 1:7). A Christian may, however, sin occasionally. John is very careful to avoid teaching sinless perfection. The basic power of sin is broken in salvation, and a Christian will not continue to sin in the same habitual way as he or she once did (1 John 3:6,8-9).

Anyone who claims to be liberated from the total presence of sin in his or her life is deceived and is a liar (1 John 1:8,10). Knowing that John often responded to the Gnostics, it is important to recall their arrogance. Gnostics not only claimed to know more but also sometimes practiced a strange "holier than thou" attitude. One clue to this connection with the Gnostics is John's definition of sin as "lawlessness" in 1 John 3:4 (NIV).

As we will see more fully in the chapter on Paul, the Gnostics could hold to libertinism or antinomianism (lawlessness). Because their bodies were bad and not really part of their essence, they felt they could do anything they wanted to do. In other words, they were above the law and above sin as defined by ordinary people. Traditional standards of right and wrong did not apply to them. John's response is that the Christian is not enslaved to sin but does still struggle with some sin.

Freedom to Love

Love is such a slippery word in English because it has so many meanings. We love our spouses, our kids, our pets, our church, and our country, yet the meaning of "love" is different in each case. Jesus frequently spoke of love, and John developed that theme in his writings. In order to focus our thinking, we'll look at just a few of the key passages.

During the night of the last supper and his betrayal, Jesus gave his disciples a new commandment: "As I have loved you, so you must love one another" (John 13:34, GNB). This commandment was "new" at least in the motivation given for loving others. The Old Testament law had mandated loving others as much as you love yourself (Lev. 19:18b) and Jesus had repeated that command as part of the greatest commandment (Matt. 22:39). Now he tells the disciples to love as much as he has loved them. They would recognize the depth of that love only after his death on the cross.

Most of us realize how difficult it is to love. We seem to be so self-centered that we really cannot love another easily. Jesus liberated us *for* loving relationships by first liberating us *from* our sins. Then he epitomized the loving relationship for us in his earthly ministry. A very vivid portrayal of Jesus' liberating love is his dealing with Simon Peter after the resurrection. John alone of the Gospel writers tells us how Jesus asked Peter three times if he loved Jesus.

Jesus began by using the Greek word for self-giving, sacrificial love (*agape*). Peter could only respond that he loved Jesus in the sense of friendship (*philia*), a lesser kind of love. Many have suggested that Jesus asked his question three times to match the three denials of Peter. Perhaps so, but for us the important point is that Jesus was demonstrating to Peter once again that being freed to love is a gradual, sometimes painful process. Just as Christians may sin occasionally after being liberated from sin, so Christians may still be unloving in some relationships even after they have begun the process of being liberated from their unloving attitudes.

John's first letter deals frequently with the command to love others (1 John 2:9-11; 3:11-18; 4:7-12,19-20). Perhaps John treated this aspect of the Christian life so much because of the Gnostic threat. Although the Gnostics could be very immoral because of their libertinism, John was more concerned with their elitism and their disregard of their brothers. Because they possessed this special knowledge (*gnosis*) the Gnostics felt they were better than others. They failed to follow Jesus' command to love others. They felt they were too good to condescend to love the uninitiated.

Freedom to Believe

Do you find it hard to accept or believe some new idea or fact? We don't have trouble believing some new things, but sometimes there are barriers to belief. John wrote his Gospel "that you may believe that Jesus is the Messiah, the Son of God" (John 20:31, GNB). Apparently, many people in the time of Jesus were reluctant to believe in Jesus. Throughout his Gospel John amassed evidence for the verdict that Jesus was the Son of God.

Part of John's evidence was the testimony of various people, including Jesus himself. For example, he recorded John the Baptist's experience with Jesus as if it were a deposition for a courtroom (John 1:32-34). Jesus' testimony to his own identity includes his works (John 5:36). The testimony of God himself supports Jesus' claims (John 5:37-38).

One of the major barriers to believing in Jesus was preconceptions people had about him. Nathanael hesitated because anything good seldom came out of Nazareth (John 1:46). Nicodemus could not comprehend the experience of being born again or born from above (John 3:4). The Samaritan woman at Sychar let the traditional Jewish-Samaritan hostility get in her way (John 4:9). Some of the Jews let their belief in who Jesus' parents were hinder them (John 6:42).

John's Gospel is full of stories of people who had difficulty believing. Probably the most famous of these stories is the pilgrimage of Thomas the Twin. Thomas had great difficulty accepting the resurrection of Jesus without firsthand evidence. He had missed the appearance of the risen Jesus to the other disciples and demanded evidence. Perhaps he was from Missouri: Show me! When Jesus reappeared, Thomas acknowledged Jesus readily (John 20:24-29).

Although Thomas was liberated from his doubts by a direct encounter with Jesus, we need to recall that the transition from doubt to faith is not always an easy one. The Bible is punctuated with stories of people of faith who wrestled with doubt as part of the trying of their faith (for example, Job, Jeremiah, Habakkuk). John wanted his Christian readers to have the joyful assurance that Jesus is alive.

Freedom to Serve

Jesus liberated his disciples for service. At first it may seem that being liberated to serve overlaps with being liberated to love others. Indeed they are closely related. Ideally Christian love should produce actions beneficial to others. "Our love should not be just words and talk; it must be true love, which shows itself in action" (1 John 3:18, GNB). Just as James wrestled with the interdependence of faith and works, John stressed the interdependence of love and service.

Probably the classic passage on service in John's writing is the foot-washing episode. John does not develop the story of the last supper but rather focuses on the foot washing. Jesus performed the menial task of washing dirty feet and then used his action as an object lesson for his disciples (John 13:12-17). Jesus knew the value of demonstrating what he wanted his disciples to learn. If you know something, practice it (John 13:17)! It would be easy to explain Jesus' service here as the action of the Son of God.

Perhaps a better clue to his freedom to perform this servant's task comes in John 13:3 (GNB): "he knew that he had come from God and was going to God" (see John 8:14; 16:28). The secret to Jesus' personal freedom to serve others was his knowledge of who he was, where he came from, and where he was going. Probably each of us could be freer for service if we had that same inner assurance. Often we waste our energies and our talents trying to change our pasts and insure our futures.

Ultimately, as Christians, we are all like Jesus: we come from God and we go to God (see John 13:3). Quite likely the best summary of John's attitude on this aspect of freedom is the old prayer:

> "O Thou who art the light of the minds that know thee, the life of the souls that love thee, and the strength of the wills that serve thee, help us so to know thee that we may truly love thee, so to love thee that we may fully serve thee, whom to serve is perfect freedom; through Jesus Christ our Lord. Amen."

Freedom of Companionship

John's Gospel highlights one final aspect of the liberated life: the freedom from loneliness and the freedom of companionship. During the night of his last supper and arrest, Jesus anticipated that his disciples would be worried about physical separation from him after his death, resurrection, and ascension. He reassured them that they would not be abandoned and left as "orphans" (John 14:18-26, NIV).

He promised them the *Paraclete,* the Holy Spirit. The Greek word *paraclete* means someone called alongside: a "Helper" (GNB), "Counselor" (NIV), "Comforter" (KJV), or "Advocate" (NEB). Jesus may not be with us physically, but the spiritual presence of God will never desert us. Earlier Jesus had affirmed that God is spirit and therefore not isolated to one locale (John 4:24). The Holy Spirit will be the eternal companion that aids us in our Christian lives.

The episode in John's Gospel that best illustrates the mood of the disciples is Jesus' appearance to Mary Magdalene on resurrection Sunday morning (John 20:11-18). When Mary realized she had been talking to Jesus, she grabbed hold of him. Quite likely she had missed Jesus so much that she never wanted to lose him again. Jesus responded, "Stop clinging to Me" (John 20:17, NASB). Mary had to learn that she would not be abandoned even if Jesus was not physically present. Indeed, Jesus gave her a task to perform rather than encouraging her to linger there.

Jesus also stressed that we are freed from loneliness because of the corporate nature of our faith. Christians not only have the Holy Spirit; they have each other. In his prayer for his disciples, Jesus accents the unity of all Christians. Their unity should be like that of God the Father and the Son (John 17:20-23). Christians will suffer from loneliness from time to time, but they can face those moments better prepared if they have cultivated relationships with other Christians.

Free at Last: Revelation

The Book of Revelation is quite different from the Gospel and the letters of John in style and emphasis. The differences are so striking that many scholars argue that the same person could not have written all five of these books. Whoever wrote Revelation, he reflected a different historical situation from the other writings of John and emphasized different dimensions of freedom in Christ.

Revelation is the best New Testament example of apocalyptic literature. "Apocalyptic" comes from the Greek word *apokalypsis,* meaning unveiling or revelation. In fact, the Greek title for Revelation is *Apocalypsis.* Apocalyptic literature flourished in late Jewish history and continued past the first century in Christian circles.

The main purpose of apocalyptic writings seems to be to assure the believers that God is with them in their time of trouble.

Normally apocalyptic books reflect persecution. The events in Daniel, for example, reflect the persecution of the Babylonian captivity of the sixth century BC. Most scholars argue that Revelation was written during a time of Roman persecution of Christians, probably during the reign of Nero (about 65) or Domitian (about 95). The apocalyptic writer used vivid symbolism to remind the persecuted reader that God was still in ultimate control of history and was victorious over the forces of evil.

There are many diverse interpretations of the meaning of the specific symbols in Revelation, but most interpreters would agree that the book had to have some meaning for the first century reader, no matter how far into the future the author looked. In our discussion of freedom in Revelation we will focus on the first century meaning as well as its relevance for today.

A Christian in the late first century might face persecution from local government officials or from popular suspicion. Christianity was an illegal religion until the early fourth century. The Roman government would, within limits, tolerate the native religions of conquered countries to be practiced (for example, Judaism). The Romans were suspicious of new religions such as Christianity because they represented a potentially subversive movement.

As long as Christianity was perceived by the Roman officials as a part of Judaism, it was relatively safe (for example, Acts 18:14-16). Increasingly, however, Rome noticed the difference between Christianity and Judaism. A systematic, empire-wide persecution of Christianity did not occur until after the New Testament, but Christians were persecuted by local officials, or by popular suspicion. In some places Christianity had such a revolutionary impact that they seemed to be turning the world upside down (Acts 17:6, KJV).

In the face of persecution, John advised the readers to persevere for the faith rather than compromise their Christian convictions. Sometimes we are so caught up in the futuristic dimensions of Revelation that we forget John's advice for the present. What should I do while I wait for the consummation of history? John did not encourage a pie-in-the-sky approach to life. The present actions and attitude of his readers are very important. The basic dilemma they faced was cowardice or courage. *Cowardice* would have been the explicit denial of faith or at least such a weak, compromising Christian life that one was not in danger of being singled out for persecution.

For example, to deny the faith would be to accept the mark of the beast in order to have economic freedom (Rev. 13:16-17). One of the most serious kinds of persecution is economic. To systematically refuse someone access to the economic marketplace can be devastating. The mark of the beast represents a type of economic boycott. If you do not have the mark of the beast, you do not have economic freedom. Christians might be tempted to deny their faith by aligning with the forces of evil just to "survive" economically.

This kind of cowardice is condemned in Revelation (21:8). In fact, Revelation is the only New Testament book that explicitly mentions cowardice as a vice. Paul, for example, listed many vices or sins (for example, Gal. 5:19-21), but cowardice is not included. The historical situation of Revelation is important, however, for the inclusion of cowardice. Being lukewarm in your faith is also a way of being cowardly. You may not actively support the evil forces, but you fail to be "hot" for the faith (Rev. 3:15-16).

Courage is the attitude John proposed for his reader. Despite the temptation to compromise their beliefs and thereby gain temporary freedom, he insisted on patient endurance or perseverance (Rev. 2:2-3; 2:25; 3:10; 14:12). John did not encourage escapism. Rather, he wanted the reader to avoid any allegiance to the values of the wicked civilization (Rev. 18:4). When the wicked civilization is destroyed, others will mourn (Rev. 18:9-10), but Christians can rejoice at God's victory (Rev. 18:20). This courageous perseverance may lead to martyrdom. Some will die for the faith, but they will be freer in their death than in staying alive by compromising the faith (Rev. 2:10; 6:9).

John promised the ultimate victory of Jesus over the forces of evil, but he also described Jesus as a lamb. Interestingly, at one point the elders announce the arrival of the victorious lion of Judah, but when John looked, he saw a slaughtered lamb (Rev. 5:5-6). Jesus was victorious after his suffering, and Christians may have to die because of their courage. John seemed to be saying: you are freer courageous and dead than cowardly and alive.

Besides the freedom of courage, even martyrdom, John discussed the freedom that comes beyond death. Although he did not encourage a pie-in-the-sky escapism, he did point to the freedom from pain and suffering in heaven. The Book of Revelation may really be as much about the problem of suffering as it is about prediction of the future. Throughout the book believers seem perplexed at the suffering they are enduring (for example, Rev. 6:10-11).

John assured the reader that the final freedom will include freedom from pain and suffering (Rev. 7:16-17; 21:4). Christians will be in the immediate presence of God and will share a transformed new heaven and earth. Although all types of Christian freedom are important, this final freedom encompasses all of them and is just as eagerly awaited by us as by the first century reader. One day we will share the liberating ecstasy anticipated in the black spiritual:

> Free at last, free at last;
> Thank God, almighty,
> Free at last!

Study Questions

1. How can you be free from the "world" without rejecting the goodness of God's physical creation?
2. What aspect of the "liberated life" is closest to your personal experience? farthest from your personal experience?
3. Is the prayer quoted on page 68 a good description of the Christian life?
4. When have you been courageous for your faith? cowardly?
5. What about the "final freedom" of the afterlife is most appealing to you? Why?

Suggestions for Further Reading

Herzog, Frederick. *Liberation Theology: Liberation in the Light of the Fourth Gospel.* New York: Seabury Press, 1972.

Howard, Fred D. *1,2, & 3 John, Jude, Revelation* ("Layman's Bible Book Commentary," Vol. 24). Nashville: Broadman Press, 1982.

Summers, Ray. *Behold the Lamb: An Exposition of the Theological Themes in the Gospel of John.* Nashville: Broadman Press, 1979.

Summers, Ray. *Worthy is the Lamb: An Interpretation of Revelation.* Nashville: Broadman Press, 1951.

4

What Doth Hinder Me?

Freedom in the Acts of the Apostles

Stories are supposed to have a beginning, a middle, and an end. I'm not sure where I learned this "truth" about stories, but I've always had mixed feelings about movies, books, television shows, or plays that did not give me a neat, tidy ending. I was reminded of this "truth" a few years ago while watching an episode of "M*A*S*H" on television. All the main characters were so desperate for reading material that they tore a book into pieces so each person could read it. Everyone was frantic, however, when they discovered that the last section was missing. The novel was a murder mystery, and they had to *know* who-dun-it.

When I first began to study seriously the Acts of the Apostles, I was similarly frustrated. Acts ends with Paul in prison in Rome for two years, preaching to his visitors (Acts 28:30-31). That's it! Luke didn't tell us what happened to Paul after the two years: Was he executed? Was he released? If so, did he travel to Spain (see Rom. 15:28)?

Because Luke's account ends here, many scholars have presumed that he intended to write another volume. Acts is already the second volume in his story, his Gospel being the first. In the Gospel he told us about the life of Jesus. In Acts he told us about the early history of the Christian movement. In the third volume, unwritten or lost, he would have told the reader about the further history of the early church including what happened to Paul.

Although this theory of an unwritten third volume is plausible, some scholars have proposed that the last verse of Acts actually concludes the book in a very meaningful way. "He preached about the Kingdom of God and taught about the Lord Jesus Christ, speaking with all boldness and freedom" (Acts 28:31, GNB). Among contemporary scholars, Frank Stagg especially has argued most persuasively that this verse gives a clue to the primary purpose of Acts. Although Acts may have a number of secondary purposes, Stagg argues that Luke's chief purpose was to record the proclamation of an "unhindered" gospel. The Greek term *akolutos* ("unhindered") is the very last word in the Greek text of Acts, and some form of it appears at several key points in the book (8:36; 10:47; 11:17).

In Acts Luke showed us how the gospel was liberated from all hindrances: racial, political, religious, economic, or sexual. The good news about God's revelation in Jesus was and is for all people. Luke had sounded this note clearly in his Gospel, but in Acts he showed the struggle of the early church with this universal message.

Luke did not ignore what might be called the *vertical* dimension of freedom; God's liberation of us from sin, guilt, law, and death. Although as a historian he focused more on events than theology, he noted several times the liberating effect of Jesus on our relation to God. For example, Luke recorded Peter's emphasis on sin as slavery (Acts 5:3; 8:23). Luke also noted that Paul's early preaching included the theme of liberation from the law (Acts 13:39).

Luke's primary theme was that the gospel is for all people. He carefully highlighted the *horizontal* dimension of Christian freedom, its impact on relations between people. Racial prejudice, economic status, political boundaries, or religious background is not a hindrance to the liberating gospel of Jesus. In this chapter we will not try to review every event in Acts but rather highlight this unhindered, liberating message. We will focus on three aspects of freedom in Acts: the freedom for fellowship or community, the freedom from prejudice, and the freedom to proclaim.

Freedom for Fellowship

Reading the opening chapters of Acts, you may be struck by the emphasis on togetherness, community, or fellowship among the early Christians in Jerusalem. Such a theme may seem odd to the typical American. Our popular understanding of freedom has so emphasized the autonomy of the individual that we find it hard to believe in freedom through a group. One of our popular songs includes the words "I want to be free; I want to be me." For many of us personal freedom automatically includes freedom *from* the group.

The Jerusalem Christians discovered that true freedom can be found only in the fellowship of the Christian community. Some social scientists tell us that our basic identity or character is dependent to a great extent on our interaction with others. Sometimes we are reluctant to highlight the role of groups because groups can make mistakes that frequently are more horrendous than the actions of individuals.

Mob violence, for example, can often outstrip the actions of one vandal. The judgments of a group can sometimes be questioned when compared to the insights of a creative, individual genius. The majority can be wrong. Many of us have chuckled at the suggestion that a camel is a horse designed by a committee!

Early Christians discovered that the community of faith can be very valuable in nourishing true freedom. In this section we want to focus on some of the key passages that stress the freedom for fellowship in the Jerusalem church (Acts 1—7).

Luke twice described the cooperative, sharing attitude of the Jerusalem Christians. First, after the dramatic outpouring of the Holy Spirit on the day of Pentecost, Luke noted the new converts studied with the apostles, "taking part in the fellowship, and sharing in the fellowship meals and the prayers" (Acts 2:42, GNB).

To the modern reader probably the most unusual aspect of this situation is that Christians sold their property and distributed it to the needy (Acts 2:44-45). Although some have called this sharing a type of "communism," the context in Acts points to the motivation or basis for this sharing: the presence of the Holy Spirit. Peter's sermon at Pentecost stressed that the gift of the Holy Spirit was to *all* believers: old and young, man and woman, slaves and free people as foretold in Joel 2:28-32.

Paul elsewhere reminded us that "where the Spirit of the Lord is, there is freedom" (2 Cor. 3:17, NIV). Today we need to learn that lesson anew: the empowering of the spirit brings freedom *and* that freedom expresses itself through a genuine community of concern and sharing. True freedom in the church today might take us beyond the limited actions of our typical benevolence committees. The early church knew one could not be "spiritually" free and withhold help from the needy.

The second summary of the sharing attitude that prevailed in Jerusalem is Acts 4:32-37. Again the emphasis is on a common attitude of concern for the needy. This concern is epitomized in the generous example of Joseph of Cyprus, better known as Barnabas, the "Son of Encouragement." Barnabas apparently established the pattern of selling real estate and donating all of the money to the apostles for distribution. A thorough study of references to Barnabas in the New Testament would reveal a quite unusual character. Our interest here, however, is in his freedom from his need for possessions. We are not told how rich he was, but we know he owned real estate and his concern for the needy motivated him to this unusually generous act.

These two texts point to two related aspects or types of freedom. First, these early Christians were liberated *from* selfishness and liberated *for* sharing. Throughout our study we will see that freedom has two sides: from and for. Too often we accent only the negative side of freedom: freedom *from* some oppression. The positive side of freedom is freedom *for* some higher cause or good.

Second, the Jerusalem church was able, at least temporarily, to eradicate poverty. Luke simply recorded that there "was no one in the group who was in need" (Acts 4:34, GNB). That is a remarkable accomplishment in light of many unsuccessful attempts to alleviate the problems of poverty and hunger in our time.

Later the Jerusalem church was the target of generosity by other

Christian groups (see Rom. 15:25-26; 1 Cor. 16:1-3). Perhaps the Jerusalem church had so many needy members and so few wealthy members that even it eventually needed help from outside Jerusalem. But for awhile the Jerusalem church was a case study in freedom from poverty.

Although Luke highlighted the free, loving fellowship of the Jerusalem church, he also candidly notes the problems encountered by these Christians. Again two episodes will serve as examples. First, the deception of Ananias and Sapphira about the sale of their property shows that not all Christians were as liberated from their desire to have possessions as was Barnabas. The problem was not their decision to keep some of the proceeds from the sale but their lying to the Holy Spirit (Acts 5:1-11). Second, the selection of seven men to wait on tables grew out of a complaint over the distribution of food to some of the widows (Acts 6:1-7).

The success of the Christian movement created some logistical problems that required an administrative solution. At times we are tempted to idealize the Jerusalem church, assuming that it had no problems. Although they were probably more unified than we are as Christians today, there was still room for tension within the community. They had a clear glimpse of the free, loving community of faith we earlier described as the kingdom of freedom, but the implementation of the vision was difficult and never complete. Some like Barnabas were able to live the liberated life, but others such as Ananias and Sapphira were still enslaved to old values.

One more passage shows the nature of the church in Jerusalem. Peter's healing of the lame beggar at the Beautiful Gate in the Temple must have really impressed Luke, for he devoted almost two chapters to that event and its consequences (Acts 3—4). When the beggar asked for money, Peter responded: "I have no money at all, but I give you what I have: in the name of Jesus Christ of Nazareth I order you to get up and walk," (Acts 3:6).

The early Christians shared more than just their money. They knew that freedom from material poverty is not enough. We are liberated not only to share money with our fellow Christians but to share the gospel with the world as well. In the next two sections we will see that this proclamation of the gospel was threatened both internally by the nationalistic prejudice of some Jewish Christians and externally from persecution by Jews and Romans.

Freedom from Prejudice

Jesus had demonstrated through his actions and teaching that his ministry was for all people: Jews, Samaritans, Gentiles, men, women, children, rich, poor, saint, and sinner. In his Gospel Luke had emphasized that Jesus was the universal Savior. While Christianity had its base of operations in Jerusalem, however, almost all Christians were Jews by background or were Jewish proselytes. As Jews these people had a very strong prejudice against other nationalities.

Perhaps the biggest struggle in the early church was to realize gradually that the gospel should be proclaimed to all people. This growing liberation of the gospel from its Jewish roots can be pictured in terms of four concentric circles with each circle representing a group farther from Judaism. The four main groups won to Christianity in the first century were Jews, Samaritans, God-fearing Gentiles, and pagan Gentiles. Luke did not attempt to tell the whole story of the growth of Christianity in the first century, but he carefully noted these key transitions as Christians were liberated from their racial and nationalistic prejudices.

The first thrust of Christians outside of Jerusalem was apparently not voluntary. The martyrdom of Stephen led to further persecution of Jewish Christians, and many fled into Judea and Samaria (Acts 8:1-2). Philip, one of the seven chosen to help distribute food to the widows, preached in Samaria and several Samaritans were won to Christ. The fact that a Jew would witness to a Samaritan was amazing, however, in light of the long animosity between Jews and Samaritans. To a devout Jew a Samaritan was a "half-breed." The Samaritans were descendants of families with Jewish and pagan parents.

The Jerusalem church may have been a little suspicious of Philip's ministry to the Samaritans. At least they sent Peter and John to investigate. Peter and John prayed for the Samaritan Christians, and they experienced what has been called the "Samaritan Pentecost" (Acts 8:17). On their way back to Jerusalem Peter and John also preached in Samaritan villages! Although Luke does linger on the conversion of the Samaritans, we need to recall that Luke's Gospel also highlights Jesus' concern for the Samaritans, especially through his parable of the good Samaritan (Luke 10:25-37). What self-respecting Jew would have told a story with a Samaritan as the hero *or* have witnessed to a Samaritan? Yet Christ told the story, and Christians were expected to take the message to Samaritans!

Another significant breakthrough for the early church was the realization that Gentiles could become Christians without having been Jewish proselytes. Proselytes were Gentiles who were attracted to Judaism and were eventually converted to Judaism. While they were studying Judaism they were often called "God-fearers." Luke records several conversions of Gentile God-fearers, the two most notable being the Ethiopian eunuch and Cornelius.

Philip was led by the Holy Spirit to witness to an Ethiopian eunuch who had been to Jerusalem to worship God. He was reading Isaiah's prophecy about the suffering servant when Philip met him. Philip used that text to witness to him about Jesus. The eunuch's question "what doth hinder me to be baptized?" (Acts 8:36, KJV) includes a word related to the "unhindered" that concludes Acts. Is there any barrier or restriction on salvation? Is salvation limited to Jews or part Jews (Samaritans)? The Ethiopian had been hindered or prevented from becoming a Jew because of his physical mutilation (Deut. 23:1), but nothing could prevent him from becoming a Christian!

Luke did not focus on the geographical expansion of Christianity, so Acts does not tell us any more about the growth of Christianity in Ethiopia. Luke has clearly told the reader, however, that the gospel is for God-fearers, even eunuchs, as well as Jews and Samaritans. Physical and racial barriers are broken down in the church.

The conversion of Cornelius involved a Roman God-fearer (Acts 10:2). Through separate visions Cornelius and Peter were brought together, and Cornelius became a Christian. Through this lengthy story Luke again reminded the reader that the gospel is for all people, including members of the occupation army. One of the most intriguing parts of the story is the portrayal of Peter's personal struggle. Peter had the usual Jewish reluctance to associate with Gentiles, especially Roman soldiers. His vision of unclean animals clearly prepared him for the meeting with Cornelius. Just as God had said none of the animals were "unclean" (Acts 10:15), so Peter learned that Gentiles are not "unclean" in God's sight.

After an outpouring of the Holy Spirit, a "Gentile Pentecost," Peter asked, "Can anyone keep these people from being baptized with water?" (Acts 10:47, NIV). The word translated "keep" comes from the same root as "unhindered." Peter's question parallels the Ethiopian eunuch's question in 8:36. The eunuch and Peter both realized the gospel is free for all people. Nothing such as race or being a Roman soldier can restrict the gospel.

When news of the conversion of Cornelius reached Jerusalem, some Jewish Christians were disturbed. They felt that Gentiles should be circumcised and become Jewish proselytes before becoming Christians. Peter defended his actions by retelling the conversion of Cornelius and concluded, "So if God gave them the same gift as he gave us, who believed in the Lord Jesus Christ, who was I to think that I could oppose God!" (Acts 11:17, NIV). Again the word translated "opposed" is related to the word *unhindered.* At this point these Jewish Christians seemed satisfied with Peter's account, but later the issue of Gentile conversion would provoke a major controversy in the church.

Although some Christian leaders such as Philip and Peter had begun to see the universal, unhindered nature of the gospel, many Jewish Christians allowed their religious and racial prejudice to limit their vision. The controversy reached a climax after the first missionary journey of Paul and Barnabas.

It is interesting that the church at Antioch, perhaps the first church composed of Jewish and Gentile Christians, commissioned these two missionaries. On this journey Paul and Barnabas directed their preaching to the Jews, but when they were rejected in the synagogues they reported to the church how God "had opened the door of faith to the Gentiles" (Acts 14:27, NIV).

This report about the missionary journey led to a heated debate and eventually led to a sort of Christian summit conference in Jerusalem. The stricter Jewish Christians (Judaizers or circumcision party) demanded that Gentile converts be circumcised and obey the Hebrew law (Acts 15:5). Peter spoke in defense of the preaching of salvation by grace by Paul and Barnabas, insisting God made no distinction between Jews and Gentiles. He was clearly reflecting his earlier realization that God doesn't "show favoritism" (Acts 10:34, NIV). Any attempt to require adherence to the Jewish law would be enslaving rather than liberating, like putting a yoke on someone's neck (Acts 15:10).

The final solution was proposed by James. On the requirements for salvation for Gentiles, James agreed with Peter, Paul, and Barnabas. Circumcision is unnecessary. James was sensitive, however, to the difficulty ethnic and religious groups have in overcoming traditional prejudices. He proposed that these new Gentile Christians accept four rules that would ease the social tensions between them and Jewish Christians (Acts 15:20-29). These rules prohibited eating food offered to idols, eating blood, eating animals slaughtered by strangling, and sexual immorality. Later we will see that the first of these rules was a major issue for the church at Corinth (1 Cor. 8—10).

The Jerusalem conference climaxed several years of discussion and debate about Christian freedom that began when Christianity was pushed outside of Jerusalem by persecution. Perhaps we can draw from this debate some lessons about freedom that still apply today. First, the primary conclusion was that the gospel is unhindered by racial, religious, or other kinds of boundaries. Christians were freed from prejudice. Put more bluntly, there are no second-class citizens in the church. Our struggle today may not be with circumcision, but certainly we still have difficulty with racial prejudice. For many of us it is still easier to send a missionary to Africa than to invite a family of a different color to our church.

Second, the early church discovered there is a pedagogy of freedom. *Pedagogy* means "education." Many early Christians must have been like Peter before the Cornelius episode. Although Peter's life had been transformed by Jesus, he still had lingering prejudices that hindered the expansion of the church. Sometimes our values are so ingrained that we do not lose them easily. We have to learn to be free, to express our freedom responsibly. Throughout the Bible we find this emphasis on the sometimes gradual process of expressing who in fact we already are.

Third, the early church was liberated from pettiness. The Judaizers certainly felt they were highlighting central issues (law, circumcision, etc.), but the Jerusalem conference decided that Jewish legalism was not in tune with the Christian faith. Christians must agree on what is essential, but there must also be room for diversity on minor issues. These Christians did not take a calculating, pragmatic approach and water down their faith. To the Judaizers they said an empathic no. These Christians were willing to call for some limitation of personal freedom, for example, in eating food offered to idols.

Today we need to be liberated from the compulsion for total conformity on minor issues and so threaten the real freedom we have as Christians. Like Dr. Seuss's Sneetches, it's not important whether or not we have stars on our bellies.

Freedom to Proclaim

The early church gradually realized that their message could not be hindered by narrow nationalistic or racial prejudices. The internal threat to the freedom of the gospel was defeated decisively at the Jerusalem council, although some Jewish Christians undoubtedly hung onto their old prejudices.

Another major threat to the freedom of the faith was external: persecution. Throughout the Book of Acts, Luke recorded persecution from several groups including Sadducees, Pharisees, and Roman officials. Despite the threat of persecution, these early Christians consistently proclaimed their faith freely and openly.

Before looking at some of the key experiences in Acts related to persecution, we should focus on one key Greek term, *parrhesia*. Various forms of this word appear several times in Acts, with one of the most significant occasions being in the last verse (28:31), where Paul was in jail yet "speaking with all boldness [*parrhesias*] and freedom." We have already seen how significant the term *freedom* (*akolutos*) is in Luke's description of an unhindered gospel. This other term *parrhesia* is often translated "boldness" and generally refers to the freedom these Christians felt in their proclamation. To use the jargon of our national Constitution, these Christians claimed their right to freedom of speech.

In Greek culture *parrhesia* was the right of the citizen to speak publicly, literally, to say all or everything. In a public assembly a citizen had the right and privilege to express his convictions candidly and openly. In private relations *parrhesia* could refer to the candor between friends who do not need to flatter each other but can speak honestly. This freedom could be misused, of course, and sometimes degenerated into insolence and insult.

This Greek term also appears in the Septuagint, the Greek translation of the Old Testament used by some Jews and Christians in the first century. For example, it is used to describe God's liberating activity in the Exodus (Lev. 26:13) and the bold speech of divine wisdom in the marketplace (Prov. 1:20-21). In Job 22:26 and 27:9-10, for example, this freedom is the boldness or confidence one has in approaching God.

Although *parrhesia* appears in several New Testament books, it occurs most frequently in Acts. The early Christians preached with boldness, confidence, or freedom. The first reference to their boldness comes after the healing of the lame beggar in the Temple. Peter and John were arrested for their preaching after the miracle and appeared before the Sanhedrin, the major Jewish council in Jerusalem.

The Sanhedrin was impressed by the boldness of Peter and John, especially since they did not have formal theological education (Acts 4:13). The Sanhedrin ordered them to stop speaking, but the two Christians insisted they had a message they must proclaim. When Peter and John met with the other Christians, they prayed that God would give them boldness of speech (Acts 4:29). When they finished praying, they "were all filled with the Holy Spirit and began to speak God's message with boldness" (Acts 4:31, GNB).

Persecution continued, primarily through the initiative of the Sadducees (Acts 5:17-18). The Sadducees were probably concerned with the Christians on two grounds. First, the Sadducees did not believe in resurrection of the dead and would not have liked the apostles' proclamation of Jesus' resurrection (Acts 4:1-2). Second, and even more important, was that the Sadducees, as we saw in the first chapter, found freedom through collaboration with the Roman government. They would feel threatened by any group that rocked the political boat in Jerusalem. When Peter and some other apostles were again arrested, their response was "We must obey God, not men" (Acts 5:29). Here in a nutshell is a basic principle of Christian freedom, the freedom to disobey bad laws.

Although the term *parrhesia* does not occur in reference to Stephen in most manuscripts, he clearly preached with much freedom and openness. His proclamation caused a controversy among the Jews and he was killed, becoming the first known Christian martyr. His boldness and courage must have had an impact on Paul, who observed the martyrdom. When Paul later became a Christian on the road to Damascus, he preached with the same boldness we have seen in the other disciples (Acts 9:27-28).

There are other references to boldness in later Christian proclamation. On the first missionary journey, Paul and Barnabas preached with boldness at Antioch of Pisidia (Acts 13:46) and Iconium (Acts 14:3). When Apollos was in Ephesus before Paul's arrival, he spoke boldly in the synagogue (Acts 18:26). Paul also spoke boldly in Ephesus (Acts 19:8). Paul was even bold when he defended himself before Festus and Agrippa in Caesarea (Acts 26:26).

The final reference to the boldness or freedom of speech of the early church is the last verse of Acts (28:31). Paul had been in prison at least four years at this time, two years in Caesarea and two more years in Rome. Although he presumably did not like being in chains (Acts 26:29), he was still free to proclaim the gospel. For Paul the highest kind of freedom was to preach and teach "boldly and without hindrance" (Acts 28:31, NIV).

As we noted earlier, Frank Stagg has argued quite insightfully that here the Book of Acts reaches a true climax. Luke had shown that the gospel is "unhindered" (*akolutos*) and can be preached "boldly" (*parrhesia*) by early Christians. Paul reinforced this opinion with his comments in what was probably his last letter, 2 Timothy. Paul was in prison, but he knew the Christian message was liberated and liberating: "Because I preach the Good News, I suffer and I am even chained like a criminal. But the word of God is not in chains" (2 Tim. 2:9, GNB).

From this brief discussion of the freedom to proclaim or freedom of speech in Acts perhaps we can draw some lessons for us. First, these early Christians experienced a remarkable boldness or courage of speech. One recent poll indicated that the most common fear in our country is the fear of speaking in public. I have always been impressed with people who can speak well in public. When I felt called into the ministry, I was very young and had great difficulty speaking in public. Surely, I thought, God has made a mistake. My reluctance to become a minister (and a public speaker) was similar to that of Moses (Ex. 4:10-12) or Jeremiah (Jer. 1:6-10).

Jesus apparently anticipated that normal reluctance among early Christians might be intensified by the threat of persecution. He encouraged his disciples by the promise that he would give them "such words and wisdom that none of your enemies will be able to refute or contradict what you say" (Luke 21:15).

I am not suggesting that all Christians will automatically become eloquent orators. Rather, I am convinced that as Christians we do have a resource or context from which we can speak freely and boldly for our faith. We are free to speak to our friends, our co-workers, our family, and others. Bold witnessing is an essential aspect of our freedom in Christ.

If this boldness or freedom to proclaim helps us to avoid timidity, we must be aware of a possible danger. For some this boldness degenerates into bluntness or offensive candor. We are free to speak forcefully and openly for our faith, but we need to recall Paul's advice to the Ephesian Christians to use only "helpful words", not "harmful words" (Eph. 4:29, GNB). Or, as he said earlier, we need to speak the truth in love (Eph. 4:15).

Second, the early Christians had freedom from intimidation. Although frequently persecuted, they recognized they were free from subservience to human authorities, that they must obey God rather than humanity (Acts 4:19; 5:29). Very early they expressed what we now call civil disobedience. Christians have always felt free to disobey immoral laws that infringed on their freedom to proclaim the gospel. Often Christians have been considered criminals in their time because of their refusal to follow bad laws.

In our time civil disobedience has been used by people such as Martin Luther King, Jr., to bring about social change. Early Christians such as Stephen were willing to speak out boldly even at the risk of their lives. As we will see in our chapter on the General Letters, later Christians were apparently tempted to play it safe and deny their faith in order to be "free."

Study Questions

1. At this point in your Christian life, do you feel you are free from selfishness and free to share, especially regarding your physical possessions?
2. Why was the elimination of poverty in the Jerusalem church only temporary?
3. How closely does your local church approximate the freedom of the early church?
4. Are you and your friends free from prejudices that might hinder the growth of the Christian community?
5. Are you bold in your witnessing to your faith? What kind of "freedom of speech" should characterize Christians?

Suggestions for Further Reading

Stagg, Frank. *The Book of Acts: The Early Struggle for an Unhindered Gospel.* Nashville: Broadman Press, 1955.

Stagg, Frank. "The Unhindered Gospel, *"Review and Expositor.*
LXXI (Fall 1974): 451-462.
Marrow, Stanley B. *Speaking the Word Fearlessly: Boldness in the New Testament.* New York: Paulist Press, 1982.

5

For Freedom Christ Has Set Us Free:

Freedom in the Writings of Paul

To study Paul's view of freedom would surprise some people. They would argue: "Paul can't be for freedom. He told women to be quiet in church and submit to their husbands. He encouraged Christians to obey pagan rulers. He even told slaves to serve their masters!" In fact Paul did say something like this. For that reason he has often been viewed as being against freedom. Certainly, if we are to give Paul a fair hearing on freedom we need to recall from the first chapter that every passage needs to be placed within two contexts: the historical-cultural milieu and the purpose of the author's message.

Since Paul wrote so many books over several years, we will approach his writings topically. In the first section our concern will be Paul's basic orientation within the two extremes he rejected: legalism and libertinism. In the second section we will see how Paul implements his basic principles in relation to specific issues in the first century. Throughout our discussion we will try to show how Paul's emphasis on freedom has relevance for us.

You Were Called to Be Free: Paul's Principles

The title of this section (Gal. 5:13, GNB) and the title for this chapter (Gal. 5:1, NIV) both come from one of Paul's most important discussions of freedom. Indeed, Galatians has been called the "gospel of freedom." In Galatians 5 Paul sketched out three major possible orientations toward freedom for Christians. He rejected two extreme views, legalism and libertinism, and offered a better view, freedom guided by love (*agape*). Although we will mention other important passages from Paul's letters, this one chapter is invaluable for giving us an overview of Paul's perspective on freedom.

The Abolition of Freedom

Paul's major concern throughout Galatians was to respond to the Judaizers, those Jewish Christians who argued that Gentiles must obey the law in order to be saved. We glanced at this group earlier in our discussion of the Jerusalem conference in Acts 15. Paul's concern was that ultimately the Judaizer position amounted to a denial or abolition of Christian freedom and a return to legalism. "It is for freedom that Christ has set us free. Stand firm, then, and do not let yourselves be burdened again by a yoke of slavery" (Gal. 5:1, NIV).

Despite his criticism of legalism, Paul did not mean to totally deny the validity of the Jewish law. Although the law cannot save you from your sins (Gal. 3:1-20), Paul recognized that the law had a limited function. We were actually prisoners of the law until the coming of Jesus. The law functioned as a child leader (*Paidagogos*) until the revelation in Jesus (Gal. 3:23-24). The child leader in Greco-Roman society was someone who aided in the training of a child. Our word pedagogy is based on it. Salvation, however, is through Christ, not the law.

At times Paul's view of the law seems contradictory. The law cannot save, yet the "Law is good" (1 Tim. 1:8, GNB). The law is not bad in itself (Rom. 7:7), yet "Christ has brought the Law to an end" (Rom. 10:4, GNB). Paul's apparent praise or criticism of the law depended on his topic. He knew the law could not contribute to the salvation of Gentiles, so he opposed the Judaizers. He also knew, as we will see soon, that total disregard of the law as proposed by the Gnostics would be wrong for Christians.

When he wrote to the Galatians, Paul was disturbed that some Christians were forgetting the breakthrough at the Jerusalem Council and were moving towards a "Christian" legalism. Even leaders such as Peter and Barnabas seemed willing to compromise the principle of Christian freedom. When Peter and Barnabas first visited Antioch, sometime after the Jerusalem Council, they ate with Gentile Christians. But when visitors from Jerusalem, probably Judaizers, appeared, Peter and Barnabas cowardly segregated themselves from the Gentiles (Gal. 2:11-14). Paul then later forcefully, even bluntly, argued that the choice is circumcision or Christ (Gal. 5:2-6). To choose circumcision, as the Judaizers insisted, is a denial of Christ and Christian freedom. Paul's attitude is direct: "I wish that the people who are upsetting you would go all the way; let them go on and castrate themselves!" (Gal. 5:12, GNB).

The Arrogance of Freedom

Paul is equally concerned that lawlessness or libertinism be rejected by Christians. This extreme view is mentioned briefly in Galatians (5:13) but was a major concern throughout his career. The primary group proposing libertinism would have been the Gnostics, whom we met in our discussion of John's writings. The Gnostics were dualists, dividing reality into two components (physical and spiritual). They thought the physical world is inherently evil and the spiritual world is basically good.

Two radically different ethical systems could be developed from this dualism. A Gnostic might argue that his body is bad; therefore, he should try to control it by a strenuous life of physical self-denial. This self-denial would aid in the eventual liberation of his spirit or soul. Such an attitude would be Gnostic asceticism (self-denial). This attitude may be the context for Paul's insistence on the goodness of creation in passages such as 1 Timothy 4:3-4. A Gnostic might argue that since his body is evil and also not really part of his true nature, he could do anything he wanted to do. This attitude is Gnostic libertinism or antinomianism ("against-the-law-ism") and is a frequent target of attack in Paul's writing.

Paul criticized Gnostic libertinism on several scores. For example, he argued that dualism is a rejection of the biblical view of the goodness of creation. Our bodies are not evil temporary dwelling places for our souls. Christians affirm the resurrection of the body, not its disposal (1 Cor. 15)! Many people inspired by this type of dualism saw the body as a tomb, but Paul insisted the body is actually a temple (1 Cor. 6:19-20).

One of Paul's major concerns was these Gnostic libertines' arrogance about their freedom. They pushed Christian freedom and liberation from the Jewish law to the extreme of lawlessness. At Corinth the Gnostics claimed, "I am allowed to do anything" (1 Cor. 6:12, GNB). In other contexts (for example, Phil. 2:3; 3:19; Rom. 12:3,16), Paul encouraged an attitude of humility or modesty, much like Christ's. He was alarmed at the arrogance of the libertines at their freedom.

We can compare this arrogance to the rebellious attitude of some adolescents who want to stretch their wings and be independent from any authority. In fact, I'm convinced that some contemporary liberation movements go through a kind of adolescent phase before they reach maturity. In this adolescence of liberation excessive claims are made and the valid liberation concerns are often rejected by the backlash of the audience. In recent American history this happened with the black movement and the women's movement. Their concerns were often valid, but they alienated many in their audience with their arrogance.

Paul was shocked, for example, that the Corinthian Christians had allowed a case of incest to continue in the community. The incest was bad enough, but Paul was even more disturbed at the arrogant, cavalier attitude of the Corinthian libertines. "How, then, can you be proud?" (1 Cor. 5:2, GNB). This arrogance was typical of the antinomians.

Paul also noted that this claim to total freedom was misleading. These libertines often became enslaved to some physical desire or habit. As an astute observer of human nature, he knew that libertine freedom is really a counterfeit. "As for you, my brothers, you were called to be free. But do not let this freedom become an excuse for letting your physical desires control you" (Gal. 5:13, GNB). Again, our comparison with adolescence may be appropriate. Some teenagers are so eager to prove their freedom that they experiment with dangerous drugs and wind up being addicts. They are enslaved to their misused freedom!

Agape and Freedom

Paul's alternative to the extremes of legalism (Judaizers) and libertinism (Gnostics) is freedom guided by love (*agape*). The Christian is truly free, but that freedom is informed and directed by the principle of Christian love. Before developing this very basic principle in Paul's view, we need to explore some other important aspects of freedom in Christ.

One of Paul's most significant terms for salvation refers to freedom. "Redemption" basically means liberation. Prisoners of war or slaves were redeemed or set free from bondage as Jesus redeems us (Rom. 3:24). Although Paul had a very positive view of freedom, it may be easier to outline his view as freedom *from* several types of bondage.

First, Paul insisted that a Christian is *free from the power and dominion of sin*. Sinners are "slaves of sin," but a Christian "is set free from the power of sin" (Rom. 6:6-7, GNB). Paul could use the slavery image here in a positive sense. A person can choose his master, or whatever will have his or her loyalty and commitment. A Christian is no longer a "slave of sin" but a "slave of righteousness" (Rom. 6:15-23).

Second, a Christian is "free from the Law" (Rom. 7:6, GNB). As we have already seen, Paul denied the role of the law in salvation. The law was essential in God's dealings with the Jews, but salvation is by grace, the free gift of God. Paul would have liked our hymn, "Free from the law, O happy condition." The libertines had distorted this freedom, however, and, as one commentator noted, changed the next line of this hymn to: "I can sin as I please and still have remission."

Third, a Christian is *free from the fear of death*. Looking to the future consummation of history, Paul affirmed the hope that "creation itself would one day be set free from its slavery to decay and would share the glorious freedom of the children of God" (Rom.

8:21, GNB). The Christian hope is not Stoic resignation or Epicu-
rean belief in annihilation but confidence in the final freedom,
victory over death (1 Cor. 15:51-57). Christians experience genuine
freedom, but the climax of freedom for us and all creation will
come at the consummation of time as we know it (Eph. 4:30).

Fourth, a Christian is *free from the spiritual powers* (Col. 2:20).
Although Christians would struggle with spiritual warfare, the
basic victory over the evil spiritual powers was accomplished in
Christ's death and resurrection (Col. 2:15; Eph. 1:21-22). As Christians we have every confidence that the ultimate power is God's,
not Satan's. Our duty is to be prepared for conflict (Eph. 6:10-18).

Fifth, Christians are *free to be sons of God.* In Galatians Paul
contrasted the status of a slave in a household with that of a son.
The son has the right to approach his father and address him in
the most familiar of terms, *Abba* (Gal. 4:1-7). Whereas a slave may
likely be afraid of his or her master, the child knows of the father's
love and feels free to enter into his presence (Rom. 8:15; Eph. 3:12).

Although Paul discussed other dimensions of freedom, we can
easily see that being a Christian is a liberating experience. Paul does
not, however, always use freedom as his major way of describing
the Christian life. Indeed, he often described himself as a slave or
prisoner of Christ (for example, 2 Cor. 2:14; Gal. 6:17; Eph. 3:1;
Phil. 1:1; Col. 1:23; Titus 1:1; Philem. 1).

In contrast to the two extremes of legalism and libertinism,
Paul's view of freedom is paradoxical. A Christian is free *but* that
freedom may be limited by some other concerns. Of course, contemporary culture may balk at the notion of being a slave to Christ,
but Paul's view of the Christian life is not libertine. Christian
freedom is guided by loyalty to Christ and love for others. Here we
will focus on the voluntary self-limitation of personal freedom out
of regard for others.

Paul addressed the topic of self-giving love (*agape*) and freedom
in several letters, but the key text is 1 Corinthians. In Corinth a
key question was whether Christians could eat meat that had been
used in an idolatrous worship. The Jerusalem council recommended not eating such meat (Acts 15:20,29). Paul's major opponents

were probably influenced by Gnostic libertines. Paul accepted the value of knowledge (*gnosis*), but he warned that knowledge can lead to arrogance while love builds up (1 Cor. 8:1-3). Paul also acknowledged that the meat in question had not been affected at all by the idols. There were some, however, who were not "in the know" and would be offended by Christians eating meat offered to idols.

Paul's argument is that the stronger Christian should not by the exercise of his freedom deliberately offend the weaker brother. To Paul the issue of meat was really a matter of indifference. "Be careful, however, not to let your freedom of action make those who are weak in the faith fall into sin" (1 Cor. 8:9, GNB).

Paul used this issue of meat offered to idols as an occasion to develop one of the most significant principles of New Testament ethics. The Christian's personal freedom must be limited on occasion out of respect for the immature Christian or non-Christian. For Paul this voluntary limitation of freedom was the most loving thing to do (Gal. 5:13-14). Love was the highest virtue for Paul, as demonstrated in the famous love chapter (1 Cor. 13). Even when you know you are "right" in the use of mature knowledge of a subject, you still must not flaunt your freedom. Such loving limitation of liberty may involve what you eat or drink (Rom. 14:13-15).

Paul was also concerned about the evangelistic impact of the use or abuse of Christian freedom. He proposed a principle of flexibility as an evangelistic strategy. "I am a free man, nobody's slave; but I make myself everybody's slave in order to win as many as possible" (1 Cor. 9:19, GNB). Paul was not becoming a chameleon who changes his basic values or beliefs when he moves to a new town. He was always firm in his basic convictions, but he recognized the value of flexibility.

Normally, one was free to eat meat offered to idols, but if one knew eating that meat would hinder witnessing, one should refrain (1 Cor. 10:23-30). Paul here anticipates an objection to his principle of limited liberty. Why "should my freedom to act be limited by another person's conscience?" (1 Cor. 10:29, GNB). In modern psychological jargon: How can I avoid spiritual paranoia? If I always try to avoid offending someone else's conscience, I may not be able to do anything!

Paul's response was that whatever we do, we should do to God's glory (1 Cor. 10:31 to 11:1). We could, perhaps, take another theme from Paul and suggest another possible response to the paranoia possibility. Paul often stressed the need for Christians to grow up in the faith (for example, 1 Cor. 3:1-3). It could be that the weaker Christian who is easily offended by the legitimate exercise of your freedom needs to be educated gradually about the full possibilities of Christian freedom. To let an immature Christian remain immature was not Paul's policy, and it certainly should not be ours!

Paul's fundamental approach to freedom is paradoxical. We are genuinely free in Christ but our love will sometimes call on us to limit our liberty. Although eating meat offered to idols is not a hot issue today for us, the principle remains valid. Many of our day-to-day moral decisions could be helpfully informed by the application of this principle.

Perhaps one example will suffice. Christians have often debated whether total abstinence or moderation is the biblical standard for the use of alcoholic beverages. Some argue that the Bible explicitly condemns only drunkenness and immoderate use of alcohol; therefore Christians today can drink. Others argue that the principle of limited freedom suggests total abstinence is the better approach.

Although Paul recommended the therapeutic or medicinal use of wine to Timothy (1 Tim. 5:23), he actually used the drinking of wine as an example of the possible application of his principle. "The right thing to do is to keep from eating meat, drinking wine, or doing anything else that will make your brother fall" (Rom. 14:21, GNB).

For Paul the mature Christian will be free, loving, and flexible. He will be "nobody's slave" in the sense of ultimate allegiance except to God and "everybody's slave" in the sense of compassion and voluntary surrender of personal freedom for evangelism and Christian unity. Martin Luther seemed to capture the thrust of Paul's advice in his famous statement in *The Freedom of the Chris-*

tian: "A Christian is a perfectly free lord of all, subject to none. A Christian is a perfectly dutiful servant of all, subject to all."

Freedom Is What We Have: Paul's Practice

Paul was convinced that Christians were free. The real challenge of the Christian's life in the first century was how to exercise that freedom responsibly. Paul had caught a vision of the revolutionary potential of freedom in Christ that is epitomized in Galatians 3:28 (NIV): "There is neither Jew nor Greek, slave nor free, male nor female, for you are all one in Christ Jesus." Here Paul is reversing a traditional Jewish prayer in which a man thanks God for not making him a Gentile, slave, or a woman. Sometimes called Paul's "freedom manifesto," this verse points to the liberation of significant groups in first century society. In this section we will look at five of the most important social relations in the time of Paul and see how Christian freedom affected them.

Before looking at these five relations separately, one general issue that relates to all of them needs discussion. Although Paul stressed the ideal situation in each case, he also recognized that the full implementation of this liberating vision may not be possible overnight. Living in an age that has grown accustomed to rapid social change, we may need to recall why the impact of Christian liberation was gradual rather than instantaneous. Paul and other early Christians seem to have had three basic reasons for their gradual implementation of the full effects of freedom. First, there was the *eschatological* reason: Many Christians expected Christ to return soon (for example, Rom. 13:11-12). Although the sense of urgency that Christ might return at any moment is a valid motivation for Christians, some Christians failed to work out fully the social and political implications of their freedom.

Second, there was the *evangelistic* reason: Too much social and political turmoil initiated by Christians would hinder the witness of the church to nonbelievers. Paul frequently noted that the non-Christian needed to respect the Christian. If the Christian was perceived as a boat rocker or agitator, he might harm his witness (for example, 1 Thess. 4:11-12).

Third, there was the *economic* reason: Most early Christians were, according to many scholars, from the lower economic classes. Christianity did not have the economic or political "clout" to influence the political process in the first century very much. Over a long period of time, however, the Christian view of freedom could have a very powerful impact (for example, in the eventual abolition of slavery).

Neither Jew nor Greek

The racial or nationalistic tension between Jews and Gentiles was one of the sources of the Judaizer controversy. The Jews disliked the Gentiles for a number of reasons, partly because the Romans were the occupation soldiers and imposed taxes on the Jews. Although the Roman Empire was under the so-called "Roman Peace" (*Pax Romana*) during the first century, the Jews rebelled several times against them. The Zealots, especially, wanted political independence from the Romans.

As we saw in the chapter on Acts the early church gradually came to the conclusion that Gentiles could be Christians without first becoming Jews. Paul was one of the main proponents of this conclusion. On his missionary journeys he generally went to the Jewish synagogue first in each town, but he described himself as the "apostle to the Gentiles" (Rom. 11:13). Over and over again he reaffirmed this emphasis on the nonimportance of the Jew-Greek distinction in the Christian faith (Gal. 3:28; Rom. 10:12; Col. 3:11; 1 Cor. 12:13).

Perhaps his most powerful statement of this theme is in Ephesians 2. There he noted again the election of the Jews as God's people in the past. It seemed that the Gentiles, then, must be excluded from God's plan of salvation, but in Christ true union and reconciliation are possible. "For Christ himself has brought us peace by making Jews and Gentiles one people. With his own body he broke down the wall that separated them and kept them enemies" (Eph. 2:14, GNB). By using the image of a dividing wall being broken down, Paul referred to the division of the Temple area, with the Gentiles being excluded by a wall from the inner courtyard.

Today "Jew" and "Greek" are not the terms we use for "us" and "them" types of relation. We do, however, have ethnic groups that are alienated from each other. Racial prejudice is still a major concern for Christianity, because the Sunday morning worship service may still be the most segregated hour of the week. Certainly tremendous gains have been made since the civil rights movement of the 1960s, but Christians can still be saddened that Paul suggested the proper stance so many centuries ago.

Perhaps a modern version of this text written in Georgia dialect will remind us of what Paul is saying to us: "You who were initiated into the Christian fellowship are Christian allies. No more is one a white man and another a Negro; no more is one a slave and the other a free man, no longer is one a male and the other a female. For you *all* are as *one* in Christ Jesus." (Gal. 3:28, Cotton Patch Version).

Neither Slave nor Free

The economic and social distinction between slaves and free men may seem totally irrelevant to us, but in Paul's day slavery was a significant reality. Scholars have estimated there were about 60 million slaves in the Roman Empire. Slavery was not, of course, unique to the Romans. The Jews had slaves, and the laws given to Moses governed the practice (for example, Ex. 21:2-11). When Paul discussed the rules for Christian family in what scholars call the "household tables" (Eph. 5:21 to 6:9; Col. 3:18 to 4:1), he always included the duties of slaves. Some of the wealthier Christians may have had slaves, but even more Christians were slaves themselves.

Paul frequently told slaves to obey their masters (Eph. 6:5; Col. 3:22; 1 Tim. 6:1; Titus 2:9). The motivation for this subservience is not a cringing fear of retaliation for some wrongdoing. If the master was not a Christian, the motivation for submission is what we earlier called the "evangelistic reason." Paul stressed this motivation most clearly in his last letters, the Pastoral Letters. In 1 Timothy he argued: All "who are slaves must consider their masters worthy of all respect, so that no one will speak evil of the name of God and of our teaching" (6:1, GNB; see Titus 2:9-10). Because the next verse refers explicitly to Christian masters, the verse we quoted quite likely refers to non-Christian masters whose opinion of Christ and Christianity would be informed by the slave's behavior.

If the master were a Christian, there was a different potential problem. The Christian slave might presume that since in Christ there is neither slave nor free he did not have to do his job anymore. Some slaves might have been tempted to take the libertine approach and flaunt their freedom. Here Paul suggested the *agape* principle, the limitation of freedom out of love: "Slaves belonging to Christian masters must not despise them, for they are brothers. Instead, they are to serve them even better, because those who benefit from their work are believers whom they love" (1 Tim. 6:2, GNB).

Contemporary Christians often wonder why Paul did not explicitly criticize or condemn the institution of slavery. Probably all three of the reasons (eschatological, evangelistic, economic) given earlier apply here. Paul definitely expressed a principle of equality that led eventually to the abolition of slavery. That this was not accomplished in Europe and the United States until the nineteenth century is inexcusable, but it would have been realistically impossible in the Roman Empire.

Two passages, however, suggest that Paul was aware that the liberation of individual slaves might have been possible even if the abolition of slavery were not. First, 1 Corinthians 7:21-23 hints that a Christian slave should take advantage of the opportunity to gain his freedom. Paul says "if you have a chance to become a free man, use it" (1 Cor. 7:21).

The larger context of Paul's thought here, however, indicates that people should not try to make rash, radical changes in their physical or economic status after becoming a Christian. Within a few verses Paul used the eschatological reason for his advice (1 Cor. 7:26,29) although the discussion has shifted to marriage.

Second, Paul's advice to Philemon about the runaway slave Onesimus contains hints that Philemon might want to release the slave. According to Roman law, Philemon could have severely punished Onesimus, even killed him. Paul suggested that Philemon at least treat Onesimus as a Christian brother (v. 16). Later Paul suggested that Philemon might even do more than this (v. 21): release him? No one knows for sure, but it is possible that release was Paul's intention. Christian masters in general were told to treat their slaves humanely and to recall that Christ is the master of slaves and masters (Eph. 6:9).

Although human slavery is not a problem for us in our country, Paul's treatment of the issue is a good case study for how he treats a sensitive subject. Slaves and free men are united in Christ; slaves are to be responsible employees, and masters are to remember their allegiance to Christ.

Neither Male nor Female

To the typical Jewish or Gentile man a woman had an inferior status. Although women had opportunities for contributions to society outside the home, overall women were second class citizens in the ancient world. As we saw in the chapter on the Synoptic Gospels, Jesus was remarkably open in his dealings with women and did not demean them at all. Although Paul is sometimes accused of being a chauvinist, when his views on male-female relations are viewed in context, he is much closer to the attitude of Jesus. As in the case of slavery, however, he did not try to revolutionize this social relation all at once. Instead he expressed the principle that in Christ there is neither male nor female (Gal. 3:28) and pointed the way towards its later full implementation.

Although Paul frequently stressed the subservience of wives to husbands, a careful examination of the context reveals his new Christian insights. To tell women to be submissive to men would not be new to the Roman Empire or the Jewish world. What was new was the motivation. For example, in Ephesians 5:22 he said, "Wives, submit yourselves to your husbands, as to the Lord" (GNB). The context, however, is the mutual submission of all Christians out of reverence for Christ (5:21). Husbands are to love their wives as much as Christ loved the church, a kind of love that eliminates any notion of bossing or "lording it over" a wife (5:25; see Col. 3:19).

Regarding the most intimate of husband-wife relations, Paul sounds amazingly modern. Although several translations are possible of the verse, he apparently tells the men at Thessalonica to take a wife in an honorable way, not with the lust of the pagans (1 Thess. 4:4-5). In 1 Corinthians he tells the husband to consider his wife the master of his body and vice versa, indicating the need for mutual sexual satisfaction (1 Cor. 7:3-4).

Other verses in 1 Corinthians 7 seem to diminish the importance of women, marriage, and sex, but Paul's main concerns are to respond to Gnostic ascetics and to stress the importance of undivided loyalty to Christ. When Paul said "A man does well not to marry" (1 Cor. 7:1) he may well be quoting Gnostic ascetics who reject marriage and celibacy because of their dualism (RSV of this verse). Paul preferred singleness because of the possibility of Christ's return and the potential distractions of married life (1 Cor. 7:26,29,32-35; see 1 Tim. 4:3-5).

Within the church Paul struggled to implement his neither male nor female principle without creating chaos. If the eschatological motive were primary to the marriage relationship, the evangelistic motive is basic in church life. Much of his advice is directed to the Corinthian church because they were influenced by the Gnostic libertines to flaunt their freedom.

For example, Paul was disturbed about the shameful, immodest way the women were wearing their hair. Their newfound freedom in Christ led to excesses in hairstyle or head coverings that was scandalous. Lest the Corinthian men misunderstand his criticism of the women, Paul reminded them: "In our life in the Lord, however, woman is not independent of man, nor is man independent of woman" (1 Cor. 11:11, GNB).

Paul was also disturbed that women were being too talkative in worship, perhaps even speaking in tongues. Although he mentioned women praying and prophesying in public worship (1 Cor. 11:5), he later insisted that women should be silent (1 Cor. 14:33-35; see 1 Tim. 2:11-12). The historical and cultural context is very important for understanding Paul's advice. Obviously, he allowed and approved of women participating in public worship and even holding leadership positions (for example, Phoebe and Priscilla in Rom. 16:1-3).

His evangelistic concern is that the non-Christian would not understand these liberated women. To allow the church to win the lost, he urged that women not be a disruptive influence in public worship. Another factor was the lack of educational background for women. Jewish women were not allowed to study the Law, and Gentile women would also need further study to be knowledgeable interpreters of the faith.

Women and men today are beginning to realize the full consequences of Paul's teaching. To quote certain verses from Paul on the liberation or submission of women is always dangerous, but Paul was definitely closer to the teaching of Jesus on the status of women than many of us have realized!

Obey the State Authorities

Paul's discussion of Christian citizenship, like many of these other topics, has often been misunderstood. Several times he tells Christians to obey the governing authorities (Rom. 13:1-7; 1 Tim. 2:1-2; Titus 3:1). These passages have often been used to justify total, unquestioning subservience to all governments. When put into the proper context, we can see that these passages do encourage good citizenship but within limits.

The most significant of these passages is Romans 13:1-7. It is Paul's longest discussion of citizenship, and it is addressed to Christians in the capital city of the Empire. The Roman Christians were in a very sensitive situation, since the Roman government could observe their behavior so carefully. When Paul wrote to them, the Roman Empire did not apparently persecute Christians. Suetonius, a Roman historian, reported that the emperor Claudius had expelled Jews from the city of Rome because of a disturbance over "Chrestus" about 49 AD. This might have involved a debate over Christ. At the very least, this is when Aquila and Priscilla left Rome (Acts 18:2).

Paul's major concern was that Christians obey the laws of Rome and not create witnessing problems for the church. The evangelistic motivation appears here as it did in other issues. In particular, he wanted these Roman Christians to pay their taxes (Rom. 13:6-7). Certainly, Jesus' paying taxes would be a precedent, although he did not mention it (Matt. 17:24-27).

Paul was undoubtedly aware that governments or authorities could become hostile to the Christian faith. When confronted with laws or rulers who attack Christianity, Christians need to recall the principle of Acts 5:29 (GNB): "We must obey God, not men." Paul, however, was writing when the Roman government was not yet actively opposing Christianity. Paul does make it clear nonetheless that the ultimate authority is God's. Even a nonthreatening Roman government only operated at God's discretion (Rom. 13:1, 6).

Christians today need to be alert to the governmental authorities. Although being a good citizen is important, the authority of government is limited. Paul's fear was that in their enthusiasm about their freedom, Christians might disregard their civic duties. Christians today may need the opposite warning, that is, to avoid compromising their Christian faith by a naive acceptance of the government.

Decently and in Order

One other concern Paul had about freedom was related to order, chaos, and form in worship. We could probably trace a development in Paul's thought in the issues he treated in his letters. For the sake of brevity, however, we will look at two broad topics: public worship and church organization.

Some of Paul's strongest comments about freedom are in response to the disorder or chaos of worship at Corinth. He addressed three issues about worship at Corinth (head coverings, Lord's Supper, and spiritual gifts) in 1 Corinthians 11-14, but we will focus only on the use and misuse of the spiritual gifts. Paul's major concern was again the evangelistic one. The Corinthian Christians were allowing their abundance of spiritual gifts to create chaos in the church.

In chapter 13 he argued that love (*agape*) is the highest gift, and in chapter 14 he argued that prophecy was preferable to speaking in tongues. Prophecy is more beneficial to the congregation itself, and a visiting nonbeliever can understand the message. Uninterpreted speaking in tongues will confuse the visitor, whereas prophecy can lead to salvation (1 Cor. 14:23-25). Paul concluded that speaking in tongues should be controlled. Unrestrained speaking in tongues can too easily lead to chaos. Here again, love is an implicit motive for the limitation of freedom, but Paul explicitly accented the nature of God as an orderly being. "God does not want us to be in disorder but in harmony and peace." "Everything must be done in a proper and orderly way" (1 Cor. 14:33,40, GNB).

In our worship we need to achieve the balance between form and freedom that Paul described. Too often we brag on the informality and spontaneity of our public worship, but in reality we are creatures of habit. Creative, innovative worship might be a very meaningful way for an entire congregation to express its freedom. Other churches have the opposite problem. Their worship is so unplanned that more form and order would not exact any real sacrifice of freedom.

In his later writings, the Pastoral Letters (1 and 2 Timothy, Titus), Paul turned more to the question of church organization. The earliest congregations outside of Jerusalem probably had very little structure or organization. What organization that existed was probably very informal and fluid. As the church grew there was a need for more structure. In the Pastoral Letters Paul gave the qualifications for church leadership and hinted at the outlines of the emerging church order. For example, in 1 Timothy 3 and Titus 1 Paul gave the qualifications for bishop (pastor), deacon, and elder (pastor). For each office Paul was concerned that the person be mature, self-controlled, and respected.

Some scholars have worried that these later letters show the early church on the decline. If we define or describe freedom only as spontaneity or informality, any sign of structure or organization would seem to be a denial of freedom. Certainly too much organization can be dangerous. We all make jokes about appointing a new committee to look at a minor issue! Some administrative structure is essential if tasks are to be accomplished. Moses learned the value of administration centuries before Paul (Ex. 18:13-26). Today we need to be careful on the one hand not to snuff out freedom with bureaucracy and, on the other hand, not to glorify freedom at the risk of losing effectiveness. Paul told the Corinthians later that "Where the Spirit of the Lord is present, there is freedom" (2 Cor. 3:17, GNB). He did not say that Spirit and freedom are contradictory to order and organization.

Am I Not Free?

Paul's answer to his own question in 1 Corinthians 9:1 (NIV) was a resounding yes. He is free in Christ and so are you and I. He realized that his liberty was not license and that love should guide it. His writings are certainly still relevant for us. Our concerns are remarkably close to his. How do we relate to other races? What are the proper roles for men and women? What should a Christian citizen do? How free are our churches?

Study Questions

1. Is there a threat of legalism or libertinism in your personal life? in your church?
2. How should we respond to the arrogance of some liberation

movements? Total rejection? Total affirmation? Critical evaluation?

3. Have you ever voluntarily limited your freedom out of love for another?
4. What liberation or bondage have you experienced as a wife or husband?
5. Is our government in conflict with your Christian freedom? If so, how will you respond?
6. Does your church have the proper balance between freedom and order in its worship? its organization?

Suggestions for Further Reading

Bruce, F. F. *Paul: Apostle of the Heart Set Free.* Grand Rapids: Eerdmans, 1977.

Furnish, Victor Paul. *The Moral Teaching of Paul.* Nashville: Abingdon, 1979.

Longenecker, Richard N. *Paul, Apostle of Liberty.* Grand Rapids: Baker, 1976 (reprint).

Richardson, Peter. *Paul's Ethic of Freedom.* Philadelphia: Westminster, 1979.

6

Live as Free People:
Freedom in the General Letters

The Burden of Freedom. That book title caught my eye in a book store and stuck with me. Normally we think of liberation as a joyous, fulfilling experience, but sometimes freedom creates problems instead of solving them. Freedom can be bane as well as blessing. If you are free, you have choices to make, and those choices have consequences. Occasionally our freedom is so difficult to handle or has such a high price that we wish we weren't free after all.

In this chapter we will look at five New Testament writings generally classified as the general letters: Hebrews, James, 1 and 2 Peter, and Jude. Scholars usually also include 1, 2, and 3 John, but we have studied those books in our third chapter. These eight books have been called "general" letters because their audiences were *not* as well defined as Paul's letters to particular cities or groups.

Although the destinations of these letters were diverse or general, each of the authors was concerned to encourage his readers to exercise true Christian freedom. The title of the chapter, taken from 1 Peter 2:16, is appropriate for all five books. Each audience was apparently experiencing some threat to their freedom in Christ. Many of their emphases will be familiar to us by now because of our study of the other New Testament writings, but a careful study of these five books will further inform us about one of the great themes of the New Testament.

Refusing to Accept Freedom: Hebrews

The anonymous author of Hebrews knew his audience was facing a serious choice between two possible freedoms. On one hand, they could hold on to the freedom they had gained through faith in Christ. This freedom was dangerous, however, because Christianity was beginning to face persecutions. As we noted in the discussion of Revelation in chapter 3, this persecution might have been promoted by government officials or the result of popular suspicion of Christianity.

Christianity was an illegal religion in the empire, but Judaism was, within some limits, legally recognized. As long as Christianity was understood by the Roman officials to be a sect within Judaism, it was not singled out for persecution. Once the Romans saw that Christians were not merely a new form of Judaism, it was very dangerous to be a Christian. Genuine Christian freedom could be hazardous to your health!

On the other hand, freedom to live a comfortable, untroubled existence could be had by rejecting your faith and returning to your Jewish heritage. Most likely the readers of Hebrews were Jewish Christians and could escape the threat of persecution by saying they were Jews, not Christians. The author of Hebrews may have been comparing the experience of these Jewish Christians to the Jews who left Egypt with Moses. They soon experienced hardship in the wilderness and wanted to go back to Egypt.

Such an "escape from freedom" attitude may have been a possibility for these first century Jewish Christians (Heb. 3:7-19). Such a decision to deny the faith would grant only a temporary, counterfeit freedom. In his great chapter on faith, the writer noted the hardships and persecutions faced by Hebrews in the past (Heb. 11:33-38). In particular he noted that some, "refusing to accept freedom, died under torture in order to be raised to a better life" (Heb. 11:35).

The choice for the reader, then, was whether to remain loyal to true Christian freedom refusing to accept this counterfeit freedom or to seek a comfortable, safe existence by denying the faith. Perhaps the brief reference to love of money late in the book points to this dilemma: Christ or comfort. "Keep your lives free from the love of money, and be satisfied with what you have. For God has said, 'I will never leave you; I will never abandon you' " (Heb. 13:5, GNB). This may simply be a general comment on greed, or it could reflect the reader's choice. Those praised by the author are the ones who refuse to accept the false freedom.

Years ago in *The Cost of Discipleship* Dietrich Bonhoeffer discussed the difference between cheap grace and costly grace. Perhaps we can adapt his distinction: cheap freedom involves denial of the faith while costly freedom may lead to persecution. Or perhaps we can revise the words of the old song, "The best things in life are free." To a Christian, in the face of persecution, the "best thing" in life might not be freedom in comfort and economic and political independence.

To help the readers make the best choice, the author of Hebrews focused their attention on Jesus. Out of the richness of that discussion we will focus on two aspects: Jesus as the fulfillment of the sacrificial system and Jesus as pioneer.

First, the author argued that Jesus fulfilled and superseded the Jewish sacrificial system and priesthood. When the reader is tempted by a cheap freedom, the author asks: Why not the best? Through a series of comparisons the author tries to persuade the reader of the superiority of Christ over Judaism. For example, Jesus is superior to angels (Heb. 1:4 to 2:18), Moses (Heb. 3:1-6), and the Jewish high priest (Heb. 4:14 to 5:10). One of the most interesting comparisons is between Jesus and Melchizedek, the king of Salem and priest of God Most High who met Abraham (Gen. 14). Because his ancestry was mysterious, Melchizedek was a clear anticipation of Jesus' priesthood. Clearly Jesus is superior to the Jewish high priest. The high priest must repeatedly make sacrifices for his sins and those of his people. Jesus as the perfect high priest was tempted yet sinless (Heb. 4:15).

In fact, Jesus completed the Jewish sacrificial system and the priesthood by combining the two in his earthly ministry. He was both the perfect high priest and the perfect sacrificial victim. Jesus' death on the cross was the perfect, once-for-all sacrifice (Heb. 9:25-27). To the author of Hebrews the sacrificial system was only a faint copy or shadow of the sacrifice Jesus made for all sins. Through Jesus' sacrificial death, we have "complete freedom" to approach God directly (Heb. 10:19). This "complete freedom" is the *parrhesia* we saw so frequently in Acts referring to boldness of speech. Here it means the confidence the Christian has in approaching God without a human mediator (see Heb. 4:16).

To reinforce this superiority of Jesus to Judaism, the author of Hebrews compares the old covenant of the sacrificial system and the new covenant. The "new covenant" concept was introduced in the Old Testament, especially by Jeremiah (31:31-34, quoted in Heb. 8:8-12). The new covenant was established by Jesus through his death, a "death which sets people free from the wrongs they did while the first covenant was in effect" (Heb. 9:15, GNB). Again, the author's main point is that Jesus is superior to Judaism. Why settle for less than the best?

Second, the writer used the example of Jesus to encourage the readers to remain loyal to their faith in the midst of adversity. Twice in the book (Heb. 2:10; 12:2, RSV) he referred to Jesus as the "pioneer" of our faith. Although that term *pioneer* may conjure up a picture of Davy Crockett or Daniel Boone, the author very carefully built a context that would be meaningful to his Jewish Christian readers. For example, he again seemed to be comparing the situation of persecuted Jewish Christians to that of the early Hebrews fleeing Egypt in Exodus. Shortly after they left Egypt they were up against the sea with the Egyptians pursuing them from behind. In the midst of this adversity, God directed the Hebrews to "move forward" (Ex. 14:15, RSV).

Identical advice was given to the Jewish Christians who saw only trouble ahead for themselves: go on, don't retreat. Indeed, the worst thing that can happen is for a Christian to turn back and retreat from the persecution (Heb. 10:38-39). A frightened Christian might think life would be easier by denying the faith, but there is no other way to true salvation in freedom (Heb. 2:3). The writer reminded them that they had suffered in the past yet were able to press ahead because they knew they had "something much better, which would last forever" (Heb. 10:34).

The great roll call of faith in chapter 11 is full of stories of Hebrews who were faithful in the face of opposition. They refused to accept a false freedom (Heb. 11:35), just as earlier Jewish martyrs during the Maccabean revolt had died rather than be free (2 Maccabees 6:18 to 7:42). They were now witnesses of our pilgrimage as Christians (Heb. 12:2). The author uses the image of an athletic event: Christians running a race while faithful Hebrews were looking on.

Probably the writer's most persuasive advice to his readers to persevere in the faith was his view of Jesus as the "pioneer." Jesus is able to help us in our troubles because he identified with us in his earthly ministry. Here is one of the clearest statements of the humanity of Jesus in the New Testament:

> Since the children, as he calls them, are people of flesh and blood, Jesus himself became like them and shared their human nature. He did this so that through his death he might destroy the Devil, who has the power over death, and in this way set free those who were slaves all their lives because of their fear of death (Heb. 2:14-15, GNB).

Jesus is the pioneer of our salvation because he shared our human condition. Through his victory over death he is able to liberate people enslaved to the fear of death. Like John in Revelation, Hebrews says that death is not to be feared. Loyalty to our pioneer might lead to our deaths in persecution, but that would be preferable to compromising retreat. Later the writer of Hebrews used two word pictures to show the shame Jesus was willing to endure as our pioneer. Jesus was executed "outside the city gate" with the common criminals (Heb. 13:12). Christians should join Jesus "outside the camp and share his shame" (Heb. 13:13, GNB). This image reflects the Hebrew practice of excluding people from the camp as punishment and humiliation (see Num. 12:14-15) or burning the bodies of sacrificed animals outside the camp (Heb.

13:11). Both of these images show Jesus as our pioneer, who blazed the trail for us even to the extent of being our example in suffering.

Wes Seeliger's *Western Theology* gives a good interpretation of part of the message of Hebrews. He contrasted two types of Christian life using western illustrations. On the one hand is the settler theology, based on a legalistic, austere view of the Christian life. God is represented by the mayor and Jesus by the sheriff, who keeps law and order. Sin is breaking one of the rules and disturbing the law and order.

On the other hand is pioneer theology, which views the Christian life as a journey with a wagon train. God is the trail boss and Jesus is the scout. Sin is turning back from the wagon train and returning to the settlement. Seeliger seems to have caught the notion of Jesus as our pioneer, who leads us in the adventure of faith. We may not face persecution today, but like the readers of Hebrews we may be tempted to settle for less, the cheap version of freedom. Hebrews is a "message of encouragement" to all generations (Heb. 13:22). Go forward! Don't Retreat! Be free!

The Law That Gives Freedom: James

The title for this section would be surprising to many people today. How can a law give freedom? Laws restrict my freedom! For example, why should I drive 55 miles per hour? Such an attitude approximates the attitude of the libertines Paul opposed. Because the Book of James is a general letter, scholars cannot be totally sure about the audience. James referred to Jewish life at several points, and he had a Jewish background (assuming the traditional view that James was the half brother of Jesus). In earlier Jewish history there was no conflict between obedience to God's law and liberty. The psalmist said, "I will walk about in freedom, for I have sought thy precepts" (Ps. 119:45, NIV). The Jews obeyed the law out of gratitude for God's gracious dealings with them.

James only mentioned freedom explicitly twice, and both references include this notion that the law is liberating. The first reference (Jas. 1:25) occurs in the context of the relation of hearing the

word (gospel) and doing the word (Jas. 1:22). James 1:22 is sometimes identified as the key verse of James because it epitomizes one
of the major themes of the book, the interdependence of belief and
behavior. "Do not deceive yourselves by just listening to his word;
instead, put it into practice" (Jas. 1:22, GNB). The person who
hears the word and does not act on it is like the man who looks
in the mirror but forgets what he looks like. "But the man who
looks intently into the perfect law that gives freedom, and contin-
ues to do this, not forgetting what he has heard, but doing it—he
will be blessed in what he does" (Ja. 1:25, NIV). The free person
hears the word and does it. He knows who he is and what he must
do.

The second reference to the liberating law James 2:12 occurs in
the context of a discussion of discrimination according to economic
status. James was very critical of the dangers of wealth throughout
his book, and he recognized that the early church would be tempted to show favoritism to the rich. He described a worship service
which a rich man and a poor man might attend. The church should
not show preferential treatment to the rich man. Instead the
church should "obey the law of the Kingdom, which is found in
the scripture, 'Love your neighbor as you love yourself' " (Jas. 2:8,
GNB). Undoubtedly this "law of the Kingdom" is the same "law
that sets us free" mentioned a few verses later (Jas. 2:12, GNB).
The liberated Christian does not relate to people in regard to their
economic status. This person is free because he has true wisdom
as well. True wisdom "is full of compassion and produces a harvest
of good deeds; it is free from prejudice and hypocrisy" (Jas. 3:17).

When James wrote of the "law of liberty" (literal translation of
Jas. 2:12), it is clear he does not refer to some vague concept of law.
He specifically meant the command to love others as yourself. This
law was found in the Old Testament (Lev. 19:18) and was repeated
by Jesus (Mark 12:31). The person who follows this law is liberated
from the use of false standards to evaluate people. While in chapter
2 James warned against favoritism toward the rich, later he warned
against being judgmental. "Do not criticize one another, my brothers. Whoever criticizes a Christian brother or judges him, criticizes

the Law and judges it" (Jas. 4:11). Probably the "Law" James mentions here is the law of liberty, the command to love others. The Christian should love rather than judge. The Christian, as we saw, is liberated from discrimination.

James defined religion early in his discussion: "What God the Father considers to be pure and genuine religion is this: to take care of orphans and widows in their suffering and to keep oneself from being corrupted by the world" (Jas. 1:27, GNB). The most startling aspect of this definition of religion for many of us is that the criteria are moral rather than doctrinal. We are often inclined to think of religion as some beliefs, we assent to rather than something we do.

One of James's major concerns was the interrelation of doctrine and deeds. He mentioned both freedom *from* and freedom *for*. Christians are free *for* service to the needy. James pointed to two groups, orphans and widows, who had been the object of special concern in Jewish life (for example, Ex. 22:22-24). Jesus had reinforced this concern for the disadvantaged (Matt. 25:31-46). But the Christian is also free *from* the corruption of the world. James was not a Gnostic dualist trying to flee the physical world, but he was sensitive to the values of the "world" that are opposed to Christian commitment.

Through this definition and other passages, James pointed to the Christian's liberation from dead doctrine. Christians are free when they put their faith into action. He recorded an imaginary conversation between two people discussing the relation of faith and works (Jas. 2:14-26). One person argues he has faith. The second person responds that faith must produce action to be genuine faith. Belief alone is not adequate, for even the demons believe intellectually (Jas. 2:19). James illustrated his point with two Old Testament examples of faith in action: Abraham and Rahab. James concluded that "as the body without the spirit is dead, also faith without actions is dead" (Jas. 2:26). Christians should be liberated from dead doctrine to a living, active faith.

James's comments about doubt probably related to this dualism of faith and works. The doubter is "a double-minded man, unstable in all he does" (Jas. 1:8, NIV; see 4:8). The doubter is unable to commit himself to one loyalty or course of action. For James the doubter was not so much an intellectual skeptic as a fragmented person, with divided loyalties. The Christian must be liberated from doubt and liberated for a single-minded dedication to Christ. James was probably echoing the teaching of Jesus on the need for a single loyalty (Matt. 6:24). The doubter is the indecisive person, the fence sitter.

In the nineteenth century Soren Kierkegaard wrote a devotional classic about being single-minded. His starting point was James's advice to "purify your hearts, you double-minded" James 4:8, NIV). Kierkegaard's essential thought is in his title: *Purity of Heart is to Will One Thing.* The Christian's liberty includes liberty from doubt and indecision.

Dr. Seuss, the writer of children's stories, has a beautiful story about a man trying to decide which road to take. For a long time he is very wishy-washy and indecisive. The story ends with his splitting his pants trying to go both directions at once! The double-minded person is often paralyzed or in bondage to this type of indecisiveness.

Another major concern for James is our enslavement to our desires. Desires are not always evil, but often we become slaves to our desires (Jas. 1:14-15). The wars and alienations that characterize much of human life and history are due to these uncontrolled desires (Jas. 4:1-2). The desire James criticized the most is the desire for money. Apparently, some Christians at this time were wealthy and others were trying to become wealthy. The desire for wealth easily controls our actions and thoughts. Several times James warned the rich of the temporary nature of their wealth (Jas. 1:9-11; 5:1-6). James was especially critical of the presumption of the rich, who planned on life continuing so they could make a "lot of money," but forgot life is brief (Jas. 4:13-15). Their arrogance was in being totally controlled by the materialistic values. The story of King Midas illustrates beautifully the enslaving nature of the search for riches.

In sum, James's view of freedom included freedom from discrimination, freedom from dead doctrine, freedom from doubt and indecision, and freedom from desire. Primarily, the Christian is liberated by the "law of liberty," the command to love one's neighbor. Sociologists have called the 1970s the age of the "me generation." Many self-help books appeared stressing looking out for yourself first. James was troubled that this self-centered, judgmental attitude would keep one from putting one's faith into action, especially in helping the needy and loving others.

They Promise Them Freedom: 1 and 2 Peter, Jude

Peter and Jude wrote in a time of crisis. Because these three letters (1 and 2 Peter, Jude) are "general" letters, it is difficult to know precisely what the crisis was. Peter was executed in the persecution initiated by Emperor Nero (about AD 65), according to nonbiblical sources. Apparently Peter wrote his two letters in the last years of his life, knowing that the threat of persecution could easily become the real thing. Jude's letter is harder to locate in history. The traditional view is that Jude was the half brother of Jesus and the brother of James (Jude 1; Mark 6:3). Because the language of Jude is so similar to 2 Peter 2, scholars have debated if one of them might have been aware of the other's work or if they were both simply adapting some ideas common to early Christians.

Although the threat of persecution is an important factor in understanding these three letters, even more important is the libertine threat. As we saw in our discussion of Paul's opponents, the Gnostics often developed a libertine, antinomian view of freedom. You are free in Christ, they said, so do whatever you want to! The law is obsolete, we're liberated, and anything is permissible (1 Cor. 6:12). Peter and Jude never gave a complete description of their opponents, but all of the clues point to the libertines. Although the libertine threat is common to all three books, we will divide our discussion into two parts in order to maintain the distinctiveness of the understandings of freedom.

Live as Free Men . . . Live as God's Slaves

First Peter was addressed to refugees or exiles in several provinces in Asia Minor (1 Pet. 1:1) to encourage them as they faced the threat of persecution (1 Pet. 5:12). First Peter, then, joins Revelation and Hebrews as part of the persecution literature of the New Testament. Like Revelation and Hebrews, Peter does not recommend violent political rebellion against the Romans. Christian zealotism would be a contradiction in terms for these writers. Christians should be prepared to endure suffering. Indeed, this suffering was similar to the refining of precious metals; it was a time of testing (1 Pet. 1:6-7). Peter told them "you know what was paid to set you free from the worthless manner of life handed down by your ancestors." You were set free by "the costly sacrifice of Christ" (1 Pet. 1:18-19, GNB). They were to live a distinctive, holy life.

Peter was especially convinced that the libertines might influence immature Christians to misuse their freedom and harm the church's witness in pagan society. Peter, like Paul, had a very strong evangelistic motive for limiting the expression of personal freedom. One key section of the book, 1 Peter 2:11 to 3:17, discusses the duties of Christians in regard to their personal freedom. His evangelistic principle comes early in that section: "Live such good lives among the pagans that, though they accuse you of doing wrong, they may see your good deeds and glorify God on the day he visits us" (1 Peter 2:12, NIV). When Peter told these early Christians to submit to all authorities, he was not encouraging them to be doormats in the pagan world. They were not to limit their freedom out of cowardice but out of a deep concern for their long term impact on that society and its salvation. The response to the libertines is similar to Paul's: "Live as free people; do not, however, use your freedom to cover up any evil, but live as God's slaves" (1 Pet. 2:16, GNB).

Peter considered several specific examples of this polarity of living as free men and living as slaves of God. First, he urged Christians to be good citizens by submitting to the emperor and to the other political leaders. He recognized that there is a difference in loyalties, for they were to fear God and respect the emperor (1 Pet. 2:17). This ranking probably echoes Peter's comment to the Sanhedrin that Christians must obey God rather than men when those loyalties conflict (Acts 5:29).

Peter then focused on family relationships. Although he was not always explicit on this, the context seems to be that family members who are Christians need to watch their behavior, knowing that the pagan members of their household are watching them. Servants were to be submissive even when the master was harsh. Peter used the example of Jesus suffering unjustly. We are to follow "in his steps" (1 Pet. 2:21, GNB), a concept Charles Sheldon developed beautifully in his novel *In His Steps*. Wives were to submit because their unbelieving husbands might be won by their behavior (1 Pet. 3:1-2). Here Peter used the attitude of Sarah as an example. Peter's advice to husbands only takes one verse, but it is quite intriguing (1 Pet. 3:7). On the one hand, a husband must recognize that his wife belongs to the "weaker sex." On the other hand, the husband must be respectful of his wife in order that nothing interfere with their prayer life. Peter probably was generalizing that wives are normally weaker physically than men, but he did not want the husband to domineer over his wife. Such a dictatorial attitude would create real problems for their prayer life.

Peter then suggested that all Christians practice a loving, non-vindictive attitude. If they are called upon to defend their faith, perhaps before Roman officials during persecution, they are to respond with "gentleness and respect," again hoping that the non-believer will be won to Christ (1 Pet. 3:16, GNB). Overall, the pagans would probably notice the changes in their behavior as Christians and quite likely insult them (1 Pet. 4:4). The pagans might be won to Christ eventually, but in the short term Christians should expect to endure suffering, knowing that God cares for them (1 Pet. 5:7).

To some Peter was rejecting personal freedom, but he, like Paul, was quite aware of the dangers of libertinism. He was especially sensitive that new Christians in the exuberance of their freedom might create problems for the Christian minority in the Roman Empire. Many causes have been promoted under the banner of freedom, but some are not compatible with the Christian faith. Christians should live as free people, but they should never claim freedom as the defense for immoral actions (1 Pet. 2:16). Even today some people are so dedicated to proving to others that they are free that they resort to immoral activities. In our discussion of the libertines in the chapter on Paul, I suggested that some teenagers illustrate the lawlessness of the libertines. Perhaps middle-aged adults going through mid-life crisis might fit as well. Some people in their forties, for example, have extramarital affairs to prove they are free. They justify their actions as expressions of their personal freedom.

The Errors of Lawless Men

The libertines are again the main opponents in 2 Peter and Jude. To Peter the most ironic aspect of the libertine position was that they promised freedom to their followers, but the libertines themselves were "slaves of destructive habits" (2 Pet. 2:19, GNB). They promised what they did not personally have! They were actually "controlled by their own lusts," so how could they help anyone be free (2 Pet. 3:3, GNB)? They distorted "the message about the grace of our God to excuse their immoral ways" (Jude 4). Instead of being free, they actually have lowered themselves to the level of animals and function on the level of instinct rather than free choice (2 Pet. 2:12-14; Jude 19). Jude seemed to be suggesting that they were really subhuman because they are so driven by their lusts. Like the libertines opposed by Paul, these people were arrogant and defiant of authority (2 Pet. 2:10; Jude 8).

Jude even contrasted their insolence and disrespect for authority with the humility of Michael, the archangel (Jude 9). According to a nonbiblical story, Michael quarrelled with Satan over the possession of Moses' body, but would not stoop to insulting Satan. The libertines' arrogance included their misuse of Scripture. Peter accused his opponents of distorting Scripture, including Paul's letters (2 Pet. 3:16). Their arrogance perhaps led to an extremely individualistic view of Scripture (2 Pet. 1:20, GNB) which ignored the guidance of the Holy Spirit. Baptists have historically stressed the right of the individual to interpret Scripture free from the interference of state or church. We must always recall, however, that the Holy spirit who inspired the biblical writers must illumine us today.

Another feature of the libertine's character is their greed (2 Pet. 2:3,14; Jude 11). Jude elaborated by using the example of Balaam, the non-Hebrew prophet who initially agreed to pronounce a curse on the Hebrews for a fee. This notion that false teachers such as the libertines operate on a mercenary level is common in the Bible. Many religious leaders have been corrupted by the desire for money or physical reward (for example, Mic. 3:5,11). Frequently, false teachers were prophets with profit motives! Paul told us that the love of money is the root of all evil (1 Tim. 6:10). It is not unusual, then, that the libertines would have this motive as well.

One of the major emphases of 2 Peter and Jude is that these false teachers will face definite punishment by God. Both authors give numerous examples of rebels and libertines in the past who were eventually punished by God. The libertines apparently felt they could do whatever they wanted to because they believed this life was all that counts. They poked fun at the Christian belief in the return of Christ, arguing that history keeps rolling on without any significant change (2 Pet. 3:3-4). Peter noted that history has seen great changes in the past, especially in the flood. Also, what seems to be a delay in the return of Christ to us may simply be a difference in our way of calculating time from God's way. The libertines had responded to this apparent delay by doing whatever they felt like doing. Their excesses would be an embarassment to the Epicureans, who at least tried to encourage a prudent lifestyle even though they did not believe in life after death. Peter asked, Since Jesus will return, what kind of people should we be while we wait? (2 Pet. 3:11,14). He responded, in effect, that we should live responsible, moral lives, using our freedom wisely.

In responding to the libertine critics of Christian hope, Peter touched on one of the most significant aspects of Christian freedom for us today. Since Jesus has not returned for almost 2000 years, what do we do? The Epicureans suggested living a life of enlightened self-interest. The libertines promoted total self-indulgence. The Zealots attempted to establish the kingdom by force. The Judaizers wanted to uphold the Jewish law basically unchanged. How are we as contemporary Christians to be free in Christ *today?* In our last chapter we will look briefly at what our study means for us today and tomorrow.

Study Questions

1. Has freedom been a burden for you? How?
2. Should freedom be the most important or "best" thing in your life? Would you have rejected "cheap freedom" in the face of persecution?
3. What does "dead doctrine" mean to you? According to James, how can doctrine be living?
4. What is the "law of liberty" in James? How could you apply it to your daily decisions and actions?

Suggestions for Further Reading

Hobbs, Herschel H. *Hebrews: Challenges to Bold Discipleship.* Nashville: Broadman Press, 1971.

Seeliger, Wes. *Western Theology.* Atlanta: Forum House, 1973.

Sheldon, Charles M. *In His Steps.* Old Tappan, New Jersey: Revell, 1977 printing.

Valentine, Foy. *Hebrews, James, 1 & 2 Peter* (*Layman's Bible Book Commentary,* Vol. 23). Nashville: Broadman Press, 1981.

7

The Future of Freedom

1984. That number may be just another year on the calendar for some, but if you've read George Orwell's frightening book by that title you had other reactions. Orwell, writing in the aftermath of World War II, pictured a rigidly totalitarian society where freedom is almost obsolete. Indeed, one of Big Brother's mottos is "Freedom Is Slavery." Is the rejection of freedom the only option for the future? So far, we have explored some of the major features of the New Testament understanding of freedom. Now we're ready for the "So what?" question. If Christ has set us free, what are we going to do about it? Jesus' advice to his disciples was, "Freely you have received, freely give" (Matt. 10:8, NIV). In this brief concluding chapter, I want to blend some of the insights from our study and point toward the future of freedom. The three section headings are loosely adapted from Paul's description of God in Romans 11:36 (NEB): "Source, Guide, and Goal of all that is—to him be glory for ever! Amen."

Freedom as the Gift of God

Ultimately, all true freedom is grounded and rooted in God. God graciously gives us freedom. Some contemporary critics of institutional Christianity might be surprised that God is profreedom, but all through the Bible God is pictured as the liberator. In the Old Testament the Hebrews were liberated from captivity in Egypt and Babylon through God's intervention. For example, God told the captives in Babylon to "go free!" (Isa. 48:20, GNB) and "Be free!"

(Isa. 49:9, NIV). The New Testament is equally clear that liberation is the result of God's initiative. As one theologian noted, God
delights in freedom. God is free and wants us to be free.

Our culture is heavily oriented to self-liberation or autonomy.
Recently I saw a television commercial for some frozen food stressing that with this product you could "Set yourself free." Fast foods
can give us extra leisure, but genuine freedom is a gift of God. The
Bible and human experience both testify that apart from Christ
true freedom is impossible.

The freedom given to us by God is multifaceted. Christ frees us
from sin, the fear of death, anxiety, the law, prejudice, and many
other forms of slavery. One real danger we face as Christians is
limiting Christ's liberating influence to just one aspect of our existence. For example, we often restrict freedom to the "spiritual" and
ignore the so-called "secular" aspects of our freedom. Or we stress
our private freedom but fail to let Christian freedom influence our
social lives at school, on the job, or in the community. Christ
liberates us from satisfaction with our private, inward freedom and
urges us to give public, outward expression to our freedom. Our
freedom is both personal and interpersonal. Or we think of freedom
only in negative terms, as freedom *from* some bondage. Christ also
frees us *for* a fuller, richer life, the liberated life.

Freedom as the Goal of Human Life

Freedom is unfinished business. Although we *are* free now, there
is a future to freedom. Freedom is not only a gift but a goal, a task.
Paul recognized that all of creation awaits the final freedom that
will come at the end of time. Paul says "we wait for God to make
us his sons and set our whole being free" (Rom. 8:23, GNB). As
Christians we are caught between the *already* and the *not yet* of
freedom. We are already free in Christ, but the struggle for the full
realization of that freedom goes on in our time.

Earlier we saw that Paul's vision of freedom for slaves, Gentiles,
and women (Gal. 3:28) was not fully implemented in his day
because of economic, eschatological, and evangelistic factors.

Christians today have the opportunity and responsibility of participating in contemporary liberation movements. Some liberation movements have flaunted their new-found freedom. Because of this arrogance of freedom, some evangelical Christians ignore or totally reject any liberation efforts in contemporary society. A more responsible approach would be critical participation in liberation movements. Christians should evaluate each liberation movement in light of the biblical witness and support those that are compatible with that witness. For example, the recent feminist movement is not totally bad or good. Some feminist writers are committed Christians, while others are harsh critics of Christianity. We need to evaluate the feminist movement, or any liberation movement, carefully and decide to what extent we can support it.

Our choices seem to be three in relation to liberation movements: uncritical acceptance, total rejection, or critical participation. *Uncritical acceptance* means we support a movement just because it says it's profreedom. As Christians we are profreedom; but we realize there are many counterfeit forms of freedom, just as in the first century. *Total rejection* means we refuse to give any support to contemporary liberation concerns. Some church groups are so authority oriented that they become very uneasy with the search for freedom. *Critical participation* is the careful, thoughtful discernment of the validity of a freedom movement in light of the Bible. Hopefully, this book has helped you establish a frame of reference for evaluating freedom movements.

The civil rights movement of the 1960s is a case in point. Many white Christians were perplexed about how to respond to the concerns of blacks. As Christians our response was mixed: we worked for full freedom for blacks (economic, social, educational) but we had to oppose the use of violence by some. We could not totally accept or reject all aspects of the civil rights movement.

One of the major challenges of freedom is its apparent ambiguity. We are free, but we have trouble defining the limits of our freedom. Like Adam and Eve, we are finite and free. We may have a sense of uneasiness or anxiety about the nature of our freedom. My daughter Karen sometimes experiences this ambiguity of freedom. She is old enough to do many things on her own, but sometimes she's not sure how free she really is. She's not as free as her older sister, Amy, but she's not sure of the limits of her freedom. One of my responsibilities as a parent is to help her grow into a free and responsible adult, aware of her freedom in Christ.

When we face the ambiguity of freedom, our response may be to retreat from freedom or to resort to authoritarianism. Some Christians apathetically refuse to exercise their freedom and allow someone else to dictate to them their beliefs and behavior. Other Christians arrogantly choose to ignore the freedom of other Christians and try to dogmatically impose their beliefs on others. I suspect that some of the apathy and authoritarianism of our generation stems from our refusal to acknowledge the ambiguity of our freedom. Although we are free in Christ, we find it easier to live by rules and regulations rather than the liberating spirit of the New Testament. "The written law brings death, but the Spirit gives life." "where the Spirit of the Lord is present, there is freedom" (2 Cor. 3:6,17, GNB).

If the past few years have seen the arrogance of some liberation movements, our decade may be witnessing the rejection of freedom in favor of apathy and authoritarianism. We may be like the Hebrews who tried to escape from freedom by returning to the security of slavery in Egypt. God's command is still to "go forward" (Ex. 14:15, RSV). In this life freedom is often risky and ambiguous, but freedom is our goal as well as our gift from God. Our goal is to be mature in our freedom.

Jesus as the Guide to Freedom

True freedom comes only through Jesus. The New Testament presents Jesus as the totally free person who can liberate us. Other people and ideas may understand some aspect of freedom, but Jesus incarnated the total freedom offered by God. Jesus inaugurated freedom in his earthly ministry, but the full actualization of freedom will come at the consummation of history.

As Americans we are often impatient with the gap between the freedom we experience in Christ now and the final realization of freedom. Our culture teaches us to demand satisfaction *now*. Christian freedom is both present and future. Our demand for instant freedom may cause us to ignore the freedom we already have in Christ.

Jesus is our guide to freedom. In his earthly ministry he gave us some basic insights into the liberated life, but he recognized that Christians would have to wrestle later with the implementation of that freedom in their time and culture. We have seen how Paul and other New Testament writers followed the guidance of Jesus in their day. Unfortunately, some later generations of Christians failed to let their Christian freedom influence their society. Slavery, for example, remained a basic institution of western society until the nineteenth century. In some churches women are still treated as second-class Christians.

Paul encouraged the Philippian Christians to "continue to work out your salvation with fear and trembling" (Phil. 2:12, NIV). The *Cotton Patch Version* remains true to Paul's intent: "I urge you to carry on with your emancipation with a deep sense of reverence and responsibility." Our liberation is grounded in God's gracious gift and will be consummated in the final freedom. Meanwhile Jesus guides us as we reverently and responsibly exercise our freedom today.

Study Questions

1. What contemporary liberation movements are you most interested in studying? What are their strengths and weaknesses?
2. How could you responsibly support the cause of freedom in your town?
3. What is the ambiguity of freedom? Have you been tempted to deny your freedom or to become authoritarian?
4. Do you have a friend who needs the freedom Christ offers? Will you share your freedom with that friend?
5. How do you respond to D. E. Trueblood's words:

Save us now from satisfaction,
When we privately are free,
Yet are undisturbed in spirit
By our brother's misery.

(*Baptist Hymnal,* 1975 edition, number 313, verse 6)

Suggestions for Further Reading

Brooks, D. P. *Free to Be a Christian.* Nashville: Broadman Press, 1981.

Hinson, E. Glenn. *Soul Liberty: The Doctrine of Religious Liberty.* Nashville: Convention Press, 1975.

McClellan, Albert. *Openness and Freedom.* Nashville: Broadman Press, 1970.

Pollard, Frank. *Keeping Free.* Nashville: Broadman Press, 1983.